Kevin Whitehead has asserted his right under the Copyright, Designs and Patents Act 1988 to be identified as the author of this work.

This book is a work of non-fiction, This is my Personal Life Story.

This book is sold subject to the condition that it shall not, by way of trade or otherwise, be lent, resold, hired out, or otherwise circulated without the author's prior consent in any form of binding.

Copyright © Kevin Robert Whitehead 2012

Chapters

1. Alan
2. Daytona Motorcycles

3. Madrid
4. Barcelona
5. 7/3/2002
6. T.B.I
7. Conscious
8. Mapother House
9. Depression
10. Friends Reunited
11. First Date
12. Coin
13. Axe
14. I Love You
15. GMTV/ Paris
16. Proposal
17. Buses/Metropolis
18. Wedding
19. Honeymoon
20. London Underground
21. Twins
22. Labour
23. Cosmopolitan Photoshoot
24. Awards Night
25. 10 Downing Street
26. Olly Murs
27. Mr Wongs

Happy Accident-Fate Not Fatal

by
Kevin Whitehead

Chapter One

Alan Salter had a mini-motorbike. We were young, barely ten years old, it was the late 1980s, and our shared loved of motorbikes and all things fast meant that we soon became best mates. He'd let me ride his mini-motorbike and this just helped my love of motorbikes grow.

As the years went by, we drifted apart. Alan took a successful academic route at school, my path was, well, a much less legal one. My dad was scared that I would end up in prison, and often told me so. Four years on, I did eventually listen to him after I realised that my Illegal tendencies were turning me into someone I didn't like, and that not many other people liked either. Thankfully, turning my back on my less legal activities brought Alan and other friends back into my life in 1995. I was fifteen and had already made a huge change to my life.

Alan was still as mad about motorbikes and excitedly told me that he would be getting a scooter for his sixteenth birthday. I decided that I wanted one too, so we could ride around together. While I waited for my birthday to arrive, I spent several months trailing after Alan and his scooter on my mountain bike!

In the UK, you need to complete a Compulsory Bike Training course before you can ride any form of motorbike on the road - and this includes scooters. My parents had lost friends in motorbike accidents, and although not happy about me taking to a scooter, they paid for my CBT course, and for my birthday, they got me the much longed for second-hand scooter. I think what finally convinced them to allow me to have the scooter was the knowledge that it would ensure I was hanging round with Alan and another scooter-mad friend Jamie, rather than the people who had been such a bad influence on me.

Jamie and Alan were both several months older than me. After he turned seventeen, Alan gave up his scooter for his mum's car and Jamie progressed from his scooter to a 125 DT scrambler bike. I loved riding pillion on it and so did Alan; it went faster than thirty miles per hour and had proper gears!

I had left school at sixteen and drifted from job to job. As I approached my seventeenth birthday, I was getting some manual work, but would often just not turn up or pull frequent sickies as I'd rather spend the day riding my scooter and hanging out with my friends. After I lost yet another job, my mum and dad ended up giving me £3.50 a day to pay for petrol. I never thanked them properly at the time, but looking back I am struck by how generous they were.

I finally landed a job at a warehouse and at the grand old age of seventeen, finally realised that keeping a job and earning a wage meant that I had not only money for petrol, but money for the obligatory drunken weekends! I eventually followed Alan's example, ended up passing my driving test and using my mum's car. My parents were a lot happier about that, but I still dreamed of getting my own motorbike. Jamie still had his 125 DT, and as much fun as riding pillion was, it wasn't enough.

It was lunchtime and I was bored. I was eating lunch at the warehouse with a workmate called Adam. We were not happy with our jobs and sat there complaining about them over our sandwiches. Nowadays I am a firm believer in fate, and what happened next helped cement my faith.

I grabbed a copy of the Yellow Pages that was lying nearby and started flicking randomly through the pages. I looked across the table at Adam and stated in a rather dramatic fashion "The page fate choses where I will get my next job and my finger will choose the company,". Fate indeed had chosen and as I looked down at the book, I was shocked. My finger had landed on the nearby Angel Islington branch of Daytona Motorcycles. I did the only thing I could. I picked up the telephone and called them.

I nervously asked to speak to the manager, I didn't know what I would say or how to convince them to hire me, so when the manager took the call, I blurted out "Hello, my name's Kevin Whitehead, I am seventeen years old, I am really passionate about bikes and would like to be a mechanic, are there any vacancies for apprentices?", I barely paused for breath!

"Actually," replied the manager - who I later learned was called Mark, "we were just talking about getting an apprentice who can fit alarms; can you?"

"Unfortunately not", my heart sank but I continued "I have never even worked on an engine but I am very keen..." There was a silence that lasted for a few seconds and then a reply I didn't really expect;

"Pop down, we are after someone with more experience, but just to see."

I had thirty-five minutes of my lunch-break left. I said goodbye to Adam, ran out of the room, down to the car park, jumped onto my scooter and sped to Daytona Motorcycles. I wondered if this would be a life changing moment. I can definitely say that it was.

Chapter Two

I arrived at Daytona Motorcycles. There were bikes and machine parts surrounding me, it felt like Heaven. I met Mark and we started talking, he kept using a lot of technical terms and kept going back to check my levels of experience, never really accepting my total lack of knowledge. I acted like I knew what he was talking about and Mark talked himself into hiring me. I thought Mark was an alright bloke, but a little bit strange or weird. It wasn't until later that I realised this was due to multiple head injuries from multiple motorcycle accidents. In light of what happened to me, I now find this quite ironic.

I was now an apprentice mechanic and still on my lunch-break from the warehouse. I jumped back on my scooter and high-tailed it back. Running into the main office, I found Dave, my manager. He was a bit surprised to say the least about my lunch-break career change. I explained about my passion for motorbikes and he sighed, telling me to go and speak to the next level up of management. He didn't seem too upset about me leaving. The management team said that I may as well leave there and then. So, without a backwards glance I got back on my trusty scooter and rode straight to Daytona.

At Daytona, I met Mark again and told him that I was available for work a bit sooner than I expected. Mark smiled and said I could start the very next day. I had no tools, no idea, just enthusiasm. That didn't worry Mark.

I enjoyed being around motorbikes, and my friendships with Mark and his mechanics are some that I treasure. I became good friends with Daytona's customers too, and even arranged biking events and trips with them. I was enjoying life; I was learning about mechanics, surrounded by motorbikes and had old and new friends.

Several years passed by, I had progressed well in my apprenticeship. I was fitting insurance approved alarms to bikes and was out riding pillion on some very powerful machines. I watched track days both in the UK and abroad on holiday too. I would ride pillion with a old family friend called Auzzie and we would meet up with other bikers. In all this excitement, I kept my friendship with Alan alive. He was now at university studying for a computing degree, and in his spare time, he'd ride pillion with me.

I enjoyed working at Daytona, it became an extension of my social life. One time the Daytona Motorcycles staff (and some customers too) went to Louth, Lincolnshire. We were there to ride fast, do some filming and push some bikes to the limit. We checked into a local pub that also let rooms, I had a few too many beers and got slightly pissed and ended up banging my head on a low, old fashioned doorway. The following day I was hungover and had a bit of a headache. We loaded the bikes onto the van and headed over to Cadwell Park race track.

I was to be riding my co-worker Des's VFR 400cc, it was a race bike and rather quick! From previous experience riding pillion with Auzzie, I knew the VFR could easily go over one hundred and twenty miles per hour! The journey to the track was exciting for me, at one point we were overtaken by a group of bikers, including a rider on a VFR 400cc, just like the one I was due to ride. It shook the van with the turbulence from its speed.

We arrived at Cadwell Park and the track scrutinisers checked our bikes over. After a short wait in the paddock, I was given the go-ahead to start riding round the track. Cadwell Park isn't the fastest track on the race circuit, but it is one of the most technically challenging. As the butterflies in my stomach lessened, I started speeding up and was soon roaring round at high speed. Previously, I had only ridden motorbikes from the back of the workshop to the front and was an experienced scooter rider. That was very different from going at over 100 miles per hour on a race track!

As my confidence increased, I started taking more chances on the track, going up the inside of other bikes and braking later. Suddenly, the VFR started making some very odd noises and losing power. I managed to pull off the track safely and checked the bike over. It soon became apparent that there was a battery problem that couldn't be fixed there, so I instead became cameraman for our group.

I stood at the edge of the track to do the filming. I was cold and couldn't move about too much to keep warm. The resulting footage was a bit jumpy and we all had a good laugh at it later. Personally, I still blame the cold!

In spite of the good fortune in my life, I felt that there was something missing. I had a great job and good friends, but something was lacking. I just didn't know what.

Autumn 2001 came around, I was almost twenty-two. Alan's sister Georgie was also at university. Some of her friends were living in Madrid to sample Spanish life as part of their course.

"How do you fancy going away to Madrid for your birthday weekend?" enquired Alan. It did seem like a good idea, and he'd be able to live it up with his sister as well as live it up with me. But I had to say no as my birthday weekend clashed with my turn to work the Saturday at Daytona.

"How about taking a sickie, come on, it will be excellent?"

"I'm sure it will, but I don't pull sickies any more..." I'd shaken the bad habits of my youth and had never pulled a sickie at Daytona. I loved my job and hadn't wanted to let my friends down.

Back at work, and a few days passed by. The idea of a crazy weekend away had lodged in my brain and it was all I could think of. Gradually the idea of pulling a sickie seemed less disloyal, I had an excellent attendance record and Madrid seemed really exciting!

I'd made my decision. I was going to Madrid. After I finished work, I went round to see Alan and tell him the news. Georgie looked up the price of flights for us, and thankfully we didn't have to worry about accommodation. Georgie's friends had said we could stay in their apartment. So, for an outlay of £63 on flights, I had a holiday booked.

Over the next few weeks, my excitement about Madrid grew. I went shopping and bought come new clothes, got my Spanish currency changed up and dug out my passport. It is a universal truth that everyone's passport picture is laughable. Mine was no exception. I had curtains. If you were a young lad in the 1990s, there is a good chance that your hair was the centre-parted curtains style. The Manchester indie scene really influenced how we looked! And even though I now had a grade one skinhead, the picture was something passport control could laugh at.

But at the time, oh how stylish we thought we looked, even the heartthrobs of the day sported the curtains look. And when I thought back to my curtained, rebellious days one girl always sprang to mind.

Jane Peart. Oh she was the most beautiful girl I'd ever seen and from the moment I first saw her, I felt something for her.

Peckham Aylesham Shopping Centre isn't where you'd expect a love story to begin, but that is where this love story begins. It was 1993, I was a rebellious bad boy, keeping bad company and drawn to celebrity culture. At the time, Chris Eubanks was the world middleweight boxing champion and he was doing some demonstration sparring in the shopping centre. I think he was there to draw attention to a community project. But as I watched him spar, my gaze was drawn away from him to the most stunning girl I'd ever seen. I idly wondered if she was with Eubanks' entourage. I didn't see her leave with the general public and thought that was the last I'd ever see of her. I didn't even know her name.

A couple of months passed by. I spent my time playing football with friends, we'd get stoned too. Sometimes we'd jump on the P12 bus and go from Peckham to Surrey Quays to swim in the Thames. The pollution didn't worry us as we were young and felt that we were immortal.

One day, me and two of my 'bad boy' friends; Darren and Gary, were on the P12 when I saw the girl from the shopping centre. She was still the most stunning girl I'd ever seen. I was then surprised by Darren pointing her out to Gary and remarking "Look, it's Jane Peart and she has a friend with her too." My heart sank as I knew I didn't stand a chance with her now. Gary and Darren both had a way with the girls; I was only really comfortable talking about bikes and football or getting stoned. Not a winning combination with the ladies!

It turned out that Jane had known Gary and Darren since primary school in Peckham, and that she only lived a few minutes away from me. I couldn't understand how I'd never seen her around the area.

It turned out that my mates were more interested in Jane's friend Natalie, leaving me to talk to her. I was rather nervous, but soon started babbling to her, in a bit of a stoned haze. It turned out that she quite liked my curtains hairstyle; it reminded her of Shane, a character in the Australian soap opera Home And Away.

By then the P12 had arrived at Surrey Quays. Gary had Natalie's number and I asked for Jane's. I had wanted to stay and talk to Jane but Darren was feeling a bit left out, and hurried us away from the girls and to the quayside. Looking back I am shocked by the things I did. I'd hate to think what today's health and safety people would make of stoned teenagers leaping twelve feet off a dock into dirty river water. It isn't something I'd recommend doing!

A few days later, Gary and I arranged dates with Natalie and Jane. Darren was still a bit moody about it all, he was the leader of our little gang and the only one without a girlfriend. But the girls stuck with us through that long six-week school summer holiday. They'd come to the quayside with us to watch us swim or just hang out with us in Peckham. I liked having a girlfriend, it wasn't just the talking, it was the kissing too!

It turned out that I'd known Jane's cousin Thomas at primary school, but try as I might, I couldn't see any family resemblance between the two. I was, as usual, stoned and studying Jane's face. In my hash-induced haze, I imagined I could almost see Thomas's features superimposed over Jane's, but then she was my beautiful Jane once more. I leant over and kissed her. My first kiss was with the most beautiful girl in the world, how many boys could say that?

But young love never runs smoothly, especially when you're only thirteen. Gary and Natalie split up and I got pressured to dump Jane. I am sorry to say that I did cave in, and cravenly dumped Jane over the phone.

I'm sorry Jane.

But that summer romance would lead to something even more amazing. With a better hairstyle on my part.

At least I didn't have curtains any more, but I was concerned with how I'd pull that sickie to get to Madrid. One of my favourite clients, a guy called Mark Woods, had his motorbike booked in for a service. He was due to take it on a track day a few days after. He'd been on the Cadwell Park trip with us and had a history of crashes. I didn't want to let him down, but I wanted to be in Madrid. I needed a way to let my immediate boss Craig know that I wouldn't be in, but how to do it without giving the game away?

I then had an idea which would mean I could be sent home sick, Craig would know about it and Mark's bike would still be serviced. I locked myself in the toilet and made myself sick. A very sympathetic Craig sent me home and said he'd look after Mark's bike as he was going to be in the workshop to work on his own bike anyway. Those words were music to my ears.

My normal Friday night consisted of me and Alan heading to Chelsea Bridge. It was a weekly destination for bikers to meet up, do stunts and try not to get stopped by the police. As this was the night before our grand Madrid adventure, we left early so that we could get our packing done. It only took me an hour to pack, I didn't know where we'd end up so I made sure that I had a good mix of smart and casual clothes and boots. I'd asked Mum to phone in sick for me in the morning too. As I listened to some music, I drifted off to sleep imagining the fun that Madrid would bring.

Chapter Three

My father is a licensed London taxi driver, and whenever I went away he'd either drop me off and pick me up from the airport, or ask his friend Brian if he wasn't available. And Dad had agreed to take me, Alan, Georgie and a friend of her's called Alison to the airport. He wasn't exactly the fastest driver in the world, but he made sure you reached your destination. Eventually.

"Are you excited then?" Dad asked me, and before I had a chance to answer him, he added "Don't you go pulling sickies again, like you did when you were young."

"No Dad! This is different." I exclaimed. He didn't look happy though. We pulled up in the taxi outside Alan's house, Alan and Georgie bounced in, as happy and excited as I was, despite Dad's reservations. When we collected Alison in Greenwich, she was as excited too. We all knew that Madrid would be brilliant!

"Have a good weekend, have a good birthday and here's some money - call your mum when you get there." Dad handed me some money as we got all our luggage together.

"Thanks Dad. I will do, see you soon."

"Happy birthday son, have a good

one."

We walked into the airport, and as we had some time to spare we headed straight for the bar. Nowadays cider is a trendy drink, with more flavours and varieties than you can shake a stick at. Back in 2001, that meant that most trendy bars didn't stock it. I normally settled for vodka-based alcopops.

My eyes scanned the bar and quickly found bottles of cider. This birthday weekend was off to a great start! We drank a toast to Madrid and the drinks continued to flow until we tipsily made our way to the departure lounge. A short while later the call for boarding came over the public address system and we excitedly made our way to the plane, giggling like sugar-hyped schoolchildren.

It wasn't the first time I've been abroad. I'd done the obligatory lads' trips to Tenerife, Alcudia and Ibiza with Alan, and even across to the USA is with my parents. But there seemed something magical about this trip, I was as excited as I could ever remember being. Even now, I am a huge fan of short breaks and recommend them to everyone.

During the short flight, and somewhat aided by the cider I'd drunk at the airport bar, I managed to fall asleep. Half a dream later, we landed in Madrid. I wasn't in a rush to get off the plane, I sat there staring out of the window, with a big grin on my face waiting for the crowds to die down before disembarking. The blazing heat of summer had gone, but even in November it wasn't cold and the sun shone brightly. I grinned and made my way off the plane.

We negotiated our way to luggage reclaim and then went to the taxi rank. This is where Georgie really came into her own. Being the only fluent Spanish speaker, she spoke with the taxi driver and judging by the laughter, they shared a couple of jokes. Me, Alan and Alison were never let in on the jokes so we suspected that we were the butt of them! Everything always looks better on holiday, and as our taxi journey progressed, I mused that even the Spanish motorway looked good in the late autumn sunshine.

Finally we arrived at our destination. Across the street were a small ice cream parlour and a tobacconist's. We unloaded the taxi, and I smoked a much longed for cigarette.

Georgie rang a buzzer and a few words of Spanish came over the intercom. Georgie replied and there was much excited shouting. The door opened and out rushed a young woman straight into a big bear-hug with Georgie. Georgie then introduced her to us as Angela. She was the sort of person who's so friendly and open that you take an instant like to them. Angela decreed that any friend of Georgie's was a friend of hers, and ushered us inside - after a hug hello each!

Cramming into a small lift, we went up to the sixth floor. Angela unlocked the door to her apartment and we filed in, for all the world looking like prospective buyers, scanning the walls and decor in silence. The suitcases were stowed in a back bedroom and I heard Alan call my name; I joined him on the apartment balcony. We looked across the road at a playground, children were still playing in the November sun, but I had a feeling Alan was more interested in the young mums who were watching their children play.

From the apartment, I heard the holiday war-cry of "Drink" shouted. I decided to investigate and was soon happily drinking a very generous measure of vodka and cola. It was strong and sent a shiver down my spine. Another person soon joined our little gang. Her name was Jess and she was a friend of Angela and Georgie's. A familiar face soon appeared, it was Laura - Alison from Greenwich's cousin. It was good to see her and we chatted for a while.

There were seven of us drinking in the apartment, it had a party atmosphere and I couldn't help but think that throwing that sickie was the best thing I could have done.

The next person to arrive was a girl called Natheen, she'd known Georgie since their schooldays. Completing the group, nearly an hour later, were Angela's brother John-Paul and his girlfriend Shelly. When I first saw John-Paul, I immediately thought he'd be the group's 'responsible adult'. I was wrong, he partied as hard as us all! Shelly was a funny girl, always laughing - even at her own jokes and quips. She invariably got everyone around her laughing too.

The drinks kept on coming. I was more used to drinking cider so the generous measures of vodka quickly went straight to my head, and from there to my legs! I could feel myself getting drunk and we hadn't even left for the clubs yet! I ran to the bathroom to dunk my head in cold water to sober up a bit, got changed into some smart clothes and I was ready to hit Madrid's nightclub scene.

The Madrid girls - as I came to think of them - recommended a club they'd been to before, so we went along. Thankfully it wasn't a long wait to get in as the evenings were quite a bit cooler than the days. I headed to the bar and spotted some familiar alco-pops. With a bottle in each hand, I made my way to the dance floor, but wasn't quite drunk enough to dance at that point!

Georgie, true to style, suddenly appeared with a tray of shots for everyone. I had no idea what they were, but they tasted vile, but they were strong and did the trick. Next thing I knew, I was dancing and laughing like there'd be no tomorrow.

It is obligatory as a young British male abroad to do something stupid that will make a great photo or story and I lived up to that obligation. I told Georgie to get her camera ready, then headed to the back of the club, about ten meters from the stage. I looked at her and nodded, then proceeded to sprint to the stage, leap on and slide its length on my chest and stomach. The photos Georgie took captured the spirit of that club night and were very funny.

The girls (and Alan) were soon besieged by admirers, although Alan wasn't too keen on the chap chatting him up though, what with him preferring women! It didn't take Alan long to be dancing in the middle of the Madrid girls. The girls basked in the attention, flirting and dancing and having a whale of a time. I drank and danced some more until the club made it clear that the staff wanted to go home. The tried and tested method of lowering the volume of the music works in any language.

We all went back to the apartment and carried on drinking. Once more shots appeared, seemingly from nowhere, and even though I don't particularly like doing shots, peer pressure and not wanting to look like a lightweight in front of the girls, meant that I did some shots. Natheen decided that she'd look after the music and took charge of the stereo. She put on a CD by a folk singer called Beth Orton. This was the first time I'd heard Beth Orton, and even now hearing her music takes me back to this birthday weekend. I ended up becoming quite a big fan and bought all her albums.

As the night wore on, most of us gave up drinking and just sat back, relaxed and listening to the music. John-Paul carried on drinking just to keep the side up! As we got more relaxed, we started talking and came up with a daft idea. To be honest, this idea is now a tradition when any of us meet up now and alcohol is involved. Yes. Drunk Twister®. We played Twister®, and as we were all at least very tipsy, this made for an interesting and fun game, with lots of stumbles and falls!

As the night wore on, someone, and I still don't remember who, decided that it would be fun to give each other massages. We were all drunk, listening to Beth Orton and massaging each other. I can think of worse ways to spend a Saturday night. Well, Sunday morning really...

Although I dozed off at around five in the morning, I got up at eight and went for a stroll around the local area. I wanted to see what Madrid was like, not just the nightclubs and bars. My head was throbbing and I was still drunk. I wandered into a nearby park and sat watching a group of lads, about my age, play football in the early morning sun. I started to doze off once more, but panicked myself awake feeling my face getting warm. I didn't want to get a suntan and tip work off that maybe I hadn't spent the weekend ill in bed!

I walked back to the apartment, struck by how nice Madrid looked even in November. I knew the typical Spanish working day included a lunchtime siesta, so workers could avoid working in the hottest part of the day. It made the overall workday longer, but I appreciated and liked the common sense behind it.

Near the apartment was a small toy shop. I popped in and bought three teddy bears for the Madrid girls who had let us use their home for the weekend. When I got back there, people were starting to wake up. I gave the girls the teddies and they actually cried, I just wanted to say "thank you", but they were really touched.

We spent the rest of the day looking at the historic sights of Madrid, generally doing the 'tourist thing'. As we wandered around, the thought struck me. Why didn't I move here too. I could come here for a year, there's nothing to stop me... I could bring my bike - I'd seen a lot of motorcycle shops and figured I could easily find work as a mechanic, the roads looked good for bike riding, I liked siestas, my family weren't too far away, this could work... I didn't speak Spanish, but I thought that I could learn it. At that precise moment, the pros of moving to Spain outweighed the cons. I didn't mention my idea to anyone, but decided to check into it, once I got home.

The evening drew closer and it was time for the London crew to head back home. Angela, Jess and Laura saw us off, kissing our cheeks and waving goodbye. We got onto the Madrid Metro and I couldn't help but to compare it to the Northern Line on the London Underground. The Metro was nicer! We reached the airport and were one step closer to home.

I couldn't help it, but I wanted to stay for one more night. I knew I couldn't, so boarded the flight back to Heathrow. As the plane took off, I thought that I had to get back to Spain. I really wanted to live there.

Back at Heathrow, my dad came through for us and picked us all up in his taxi. As I sat in the back of the cab, falling into a sleep after the weekend's excitement, I heard Dad say "Worth the sickie then?", I was too tired to reply, but in my head I answered "Well worth it."

Chapter Four

I had barely got unpacked before I was researching Spanish language courses at colleges in Spain. I was surprised at how many colleges were offering the sort of course I wanted, but the one that caught my eye was the Don Quijote Language School. As I researched into the company, I found that it offered a wide variety of courses and focused on which would suit me best. I decided that the month long intensive course with accommodation would be the best one for me. But I wanted to think about it first before talking to anyone.

After a couple of weeks of deep reflection on the weekend away, potential pitfalls and benefits, I decided to speak to Craig about my idea. I had expected him to pour cold water on my idea, but he surprised me. Craig not only encouraged me to seize the moment and go, but he told me about his time living in Barcelona. He regretted not staying there for as long as he could have and said that if he could do it again, he'd have stayed out there.

I asked Craig what he'd done in Barcelona, and he told me about him and a friend. They'd spent a year out there, riding their bikes through the countryside and exploring. To earn money, they'd worked for an English company as road menders, filling potholes in the hot sun. Craig turned and looked at me, "Go now, don't wait. Take a phrase book and be gone!" This was what I wanted and needed to hear. I had at least one supporter for my crazy plan.

That night, I went to see Alan. As I explained about my idea and the research I'd already done, he looked more and more shocked. I had never been the one to suggest doing something so outrageous or impulsive. In all the groups of friends I'd had, I was never the leader, I was the one to go along with other people. We had been best mates for years and looking back, I think he was worried about losing our friendship. "I might join you after my degree..." he ventured, but I doubted that he would. He wasn't the sort of person to do something like that.

The biggest test came when breaking my news to my parents. I had been waiting for the right moment and ended up just blurting out "I'm thinking of moving to Spain, learning basic Spanish and floating around fixing scooters or labouring, whatever is available." My parents were stunned as they had no inkling of what I'd been doing. Then came all the questions about language barriers, money, losing my job at Daytona, and a million other things. I think they thought that this was just a whimsical fancy and that I needed a reality check.

I explained that I'd researched language schools, I had done my budgeting and that Craig had not only given me the benefit of his experience, had promised to keep my job open for six months in case things didn't work out in Spain and had also given me a contact for an English company in Spain so I could earn a living there. My parents looked relieved that I had thought this adventure through. My mum said "I think as long as you remember not to be too proud to come back if it doesn't work, then go for it." Their acceptance was a lovely thing to hear, and my dad added, "Just remember your break to Madrid might have been nice, but living there's another thing." They were wise words and I heeded them.

The next person I wanted to tell was my nan. The 'old girl' as we'd affectionately nick-named her was a woman who I not only loved and respected, but also viewed as a friend. I decided to go and see her the following day.

On the Sunday, I woke up and decided to check course availability at Don Quijote Language School. I decided on a course start date of thirty-first of March 2002. I emailed the college to tell them my decision and to ask if I could arrive a couple of weeks early, to get a real feel of Spain.

After sending the email off, I got ready to go and see Nan. She was pleased to see me and before I knew it, I was seated in the living room with a cup of tea and some Maria biscuits (sometimes called Marie biscuits). They were my favourite biscuit and oddly enough were a traditional Spanish biscuit. It seems like Spanish influences were everywhere! I hadn't seen Nan for a few days and she was keen to hear about my holiday. I gave her the edited highlights - she didn't really need to hear about her grandson being quite so drunk or stage-sliding!

"It sounds like you had a fantastic time." she laughed.

"Yes Nan, I did." I replied, adding "I am thinking of going and living there for a couple of years, learning `Spanish at college for the first month."

Nan looked astonished by my decision, I don't think she was too happy but I explained about my plans and what had been arranged. My planning seemed to mollify her and she gave me her seal of approval with a grandmotherly "Be careful." We then chatted about other things, and when I left, it was without a worried weight on my shoulders.

Monday morning soon came around. I woke up earlier than normal and was definitely bright-eyed and bushy-tailed. I left early for work and took a ride around the area, almost like a pre-emptive goodbye. My thoughts turned - not unsurprisingly - to Spain and I wondered if I'd miss London. I concluded, probably not.

By now, it was early December and people were decorating their shops and homes for Christmas. I wondered if people in Barcelona celebrated Christmas in the same way, was Father Christmas still a big part of the holiday or was it more religious? Well, next Christmas, I'd be in Barcelona and would find out for myself.

I got to Daytona Motorcycles and started telling my workmates about my plans - they were almost as excited as me. They were all encouraging me and wishing me luck. It was a great feeling to be so supported. A few of them had spent time travelling and thought it was a great idea to live abroad for a while. When Craig got in, I told him about the dates I'd asked Don Quijote for. He was very pleased for me and said he'd get the company contacts he'd promised me.

When I got home that night, I logged into my email account. There was a message from Don Quijote Language School. They were confirming my place on the intensive one-month course from 31st March 2002 and the two-week accommodation in advance of the course beginning. I was so happy I nearly screamed! I looked at maps of the area, deciding on the best routes and then booked my ferry crossing. I booked a single trip, a return ticket was not needed, for the 11th March. I replied to Don Quijote, requesting a single room accommodation in a shared flat, plus secure parking for my bike. I now had about three months to get everything sorted out for the adventure of a lifetime!

I love motorbikes and riding, I realised that Barcelona was near the Catalunya race track, and Madrid was home to the Jarama rack track. I was very excited about the prospect of riding those tracks, as well as biking across Spain. I definitely had to make sure I took my one-piece racing leathers. They aren't the lightest of clothes, but are essential for biking safety. Without them it was extremely unlikely that I'd be allowed to ride on any race track. This lead my mind to the practical issues of luggage and transporting everything I needed on my bike. I needed to talk to Princess.

Princess's real name was Andy, I called Princess because he had long hair. The South-African worked in Daytona's accessories department, and was the best person to speak to about luggage. On his recommendation, I bought a 'speed hump' luggage system. These fitted over the rear seat, but meant that I couldn't carry a pillion rider. But I got a really good discount on it! Now all I needed were clothes to go in the speed hump. Daytona had a motorcycle clothing department, But I needed casual clothing and didn't really have time to go shopping. "Hmmm," I thought to myself, "maybe it's time for a transfer."

After speaking to Craig, and getting him to speak to a few other managers, I was soon transferred into the clothing, accessories and parts department. I was so caught up in my preparations for Spain, that it took me completely by surprise when I realised that it was the week before Christmas. I still had to do the Christmas shopping for my family and friends. I hit the West End of London and got what I thought people would like, I even ended up getting a PlayStation 2® for Alan, as I knew I'd miss him and felt a little bit guilty about leaving him behind. At that point they were still quite new on the market and I was lucky to get hold of one!

Christmas is a time of copious alcohol consumption and Georgie decided to keep traditions alive by suggesting a pre-Christmas drink-up. That sounded good to me, the whole gang would be together and I could share my news. I just hoped that she'd forgo the trays of shots this time!

The Auctioneers in Greenwich was the chosen pub, its clients could sometimes be described as poseurs, but it was a good venue nonetheless. It was a couple of nights before Christmas and the pub was packed, groups on works do's as well as large groups of friends. It was loud and rowdy, but generally good natured. There was a group of builders nearby and one had been pestering Georgie. Her boyfriend, a nice bloke called Ben who I'd been chatting to, had a quiet word with the builder and he backed off, he wasn't happy about it though.

A short while later, I was standing on my own waiting for Alan who was in the toilets. A man came up to me thinking I was Georgie's boyfriend, mistaking me for Ben. Before I knew it, he had punched me (I think in revenge for Ben telling his mate to leave Georgie alone) and I had retaliated, punching him hard before grabbing Ben, telling him to get the girls and leave. I didn't want them mixed up in this.

As I stood outside the pub with blood spilling down my face - the bouncers having intervened and thrown me out, the police arrived. As did an ambulance. It seemed that my one punch in self-defense had floored my attacker and he needed hospital treatment. As he was in a worse state than me, I was seen as the aggressor and arrested. As I sat in the back of the police van thoughts of not being able to go to Spain flashed through my mind. What if the guy died? I could be a murderer...

At the police station, they asked me if there was anyone they should call. I said no, I didn't want to worry my parents. I gave my statement, hoping there would be CCTV footage to back my story up, and was then taken to the cells. I lay down on the tiny bunk and drifted off to sleep. An hour or so later, I was woken by a police officer telling me that my parents had arrived. "I said not to bother them..." I was quite angry, but the policeman replied that they hadn't. As I walked out to meet them, I saw that Alan was with them. All three looked scared for me but Mum and Dad asked how I was, rather than what have you done, so I assumed Alan had told them what had happened.

I was allowed to go home after the desk sergeant explained that I would have to return within fourteen days once the CCTV footage had been examined. Dad took me to the Accident and Emergency department of the local hospital, after dropping Mum off home. It turned out that my nose was broken and I needed stitches. Not a good look at Christmas, or any other time really...

A few days later, I get a call from the local police station. They had reviewed the CCTV footage of the fight, my attacker had withdrawn his allegation and they suggested that I withdraw mine against him. After a long conversation and to draw a line under the whole affair, I accepted a caution - despite feeling that this was undeserved as I was the victim in this. But it meant I could now focus on Spain once more.

To help get a grounding in speaking Spanish, I had bought myself some 'teach yourself Spanish' CDs and spent an hour or two listening to them every night. I also played an online racing game called GP500 and some of the other gamers were Spanish, so I practiced my language skills with them. I also frequented chatrooms where I could chat online in Spanish.

January flew by and I was running out of time to get everything organised. I worked at the Alexandra Palace bike show and got a lot of useful advice from other bikers. February flew by just as quickly and then it really sunk in. I was moving abroad to live, on my own with no immediate family with me for back up and support. This was something I was doing on my own. The butterflies in my stomach took up permanent residence.

Suddenly it was March. I was leaving on the eleventh of the month. Then my worrying turned into full-blown nervousness! I was worried that I'd forget all the Spanish I'd learnt, I was worried that I'd forgotten something, I was just worried. Some suppliers that Daytona did business with gave me details of Spanish stockists and suppliers, customers wished me well. Even Mark Woods offered his place in Malaga to stay at.

Home and work distracted me with leaving parties. The works' party took place in The Harp. It was a bit of an old man's pub, but at least that meant no risk of my nose being broken again! I did get a bit teary and emotional saying goodbye to the works team who had taken on a seventeen-year old apprentice with no clue but plenty of enthusiasm. My family, neighbours and friends came to mine for goodbye drinks. It was good to see everyone, and I was sad to go and leave them but my mind was made up. I was going to Spain.

I remember thinking to myself "Today is the 7th March 2002, it's a Thursday and in three day's time, I leave England for a new life in Spain."

Seven is my lucky number. All the books and mystical experts say so. I'd had a notion that my lucky number was twenty-five, but when you think about it, two and five equal seven. And certainly, 7th March 2002 is the day that changed my life.

Chapter Five

I only had a few days to finish up my business before I moved to Spain. I had to go to Daytona Motorcycles to pick up some money that was owed to me by a friend, and take one last chance to say goodbye to everyone. I jumped on my bike for the relatively short ride there.

I shared a garage with Auzzie, and as usual pulled my bike out, started it up and let it warm up while I had a quick fag. Taking my usual route to Angel Islington, I crossed the Peckham river bridge, passed along the side of Burgess Park before hitting the Old Kent Road. Part of my journey took me past the Thomas A Becket pub. It had a gym upstairs where the boxer Henry Cooper used to train.

Filtering through some traffic lights, I noticed a lorry to my right and a scooter behind me. The lorry pulled ahead and so did I, the lorry gave no indication of turning but it did. It turned left, directly into my path. Directly into me.

I didn't make it to Daytona. I didn't make it to Spain. I don't even remember that day. Or the next few days and weeks. What follows is from people telling me what happened; family, friends, medical staff, the police and witnesses.

Witness statement from the scooter rider:

> The lorry slowed down and as we both proceeded along on the inside at a slow speed, the lorry then just turned left into Kinglake Street. No signal was given of the left turn by way of hand or indicator, there was no left hand wing mirror on the lorry.
>
> The lorry hit the motorbike and then mounted the pavement. There was a loud crack as the blue/white Suzuki motorbike was struck by the side of the lorry cab, I struggled to avoid colliding with the lorry with my scooter. The rider landed on his head in the road. The lorry then stopped, then the cars' horns started. Some cars drove around the rider's body, some stopped.

From what I was told after, the scooter rider (I still don't remember his name), ran over to check on me and saw that although I was breathing - albeit noisily, I was unconscious and bleeding from my mouth. My breathing got shallower and I was struggling for breath. The scooter rider did the right thing - he did not remove my helmet. If a biker has come off their bike and there is even the slightest chance that a spinal injury could have occurred, the worst thing you can do is remove their helmet - it could be the only thing holding their neck together and the movement from removing it could cause permanent paralysis.

The police arrived within minutes, diverting traffic and arranging for an ambulance. All police are trained in first aid, and the officer could see that I was in a bad way.

The first medic on the scene was a quick response paramedic; ironically enough, they travel by motorbike. He took one look at me and got on the radio requesting that the air ambulance attend the scene as he felt that time was of the essence in saving my life. The police made space in the traffic for the helicopter to land, they also diverted traffic away from the Old Kent Road, it was already gridlocked. By sheer coincidence, a friend of mine was caught up in the traffic chaos. "Typical" he later joked with me.

The air ambulance arrived and the paramedic team jumped out and ran over to me. They talked with the first responder while doing more tests on me. I was still managing to breathe unaided, but I had no physical reflexes. You know when you tap just below your knee, your leg twitches. It's an automatic response - a reflex, it is something you have no control over, something your brain does on its own. My brain wasn't responding to the stimulus. It was clear to the medical crew, that I had some brain injury and swelling of the brain. It was too risky to take me to hospital by air, they didn't think I could cope with, or even survive the tiny change in air pressure. They radioed for an ambulance. When it arrived and I was safely on board, the ambulance received a police escort to the hospital, the sirens clearing the roads ahead.

If it was not for the expert first aid awareness of the scooter rider and police, and the expertise and professionalism of the paramedics, I would not have survived long enough to even get to the hospital. To these people, and the medical team at King's College Hospital who ensured I lived, you have my undying thanks and respect.

In the casualty unit of King's College Hospital, the medical team expertly removed my crash helmet and cleared my windpipe of any obstructions whilst another nurse cleaned and dressed a small cut on my ankle. I was taken for an MRI (magnetic resonance imaging) brain scan. This would give the doctors the information they needed about the severity of my brain injuries.

The police had used the ID in my wallet to track down my parents. Two officers arrived at my mum's work. She later said that when they'd asked for her and then asked if she was my mother, that she thought I was dead. My death was her greatest worry she'd had since I started riding scooters. Her boss walked over and just said to get in the police car and go to the hospital.

Mum tried ringing Dad on his mobile phone, but he was driving his taxi, and safety conscious as always, he wouldn't answer the phone whilst driving. She phoned my sister, and briefly explained what had happened, where I was and asked her to get in touch with Dad. She then left with the police.

When Mum arrived at King's College Hospital, the nurses took her through to the room where I was lying, hooked up to machines with myriad tubes. I'm sure that I looked more dead than alive. The last time Mum had seen me in hospital was when I was a child and had broken my arm, I been rollerskating and taken a tumble. This time, it was much more serious.

The doctor in charge of my case introduced himself to Mum and explained they were waiting for the result of the MRI scan to come through. He added the tubes were to help with my breathing, ensuring a constant flow of oxygen to my system. I later learned that my mum cried, looking at me lying there and as still as the grave.

She took some time to collect herself and get her emotions back under control, before calling Dad again. This time, he answered the call. Mum told him where she was and why. It didn't take long before Dad's taxi was parked outside the hospital and he was standing in the casualty department, holding my mum close and looking at me. He later said that the sight of me lying there, looking virtually unscathed yet hooked up to machines made him think the worst, that all the damage was hidden deep inside me. Which it was.

The doctor re-appeared and this time he had the results of the MRI scan. There was good and bad news; the good news was that there was no bleeding in the brain, all the blood vessels were intact. The bad news was that my brain was severely swollen, pushing against my skull and until the swelling went down, he could not give any diagnosis or prognosis. Mum went outside and smoked a cigarette. My dad came the closest to smoking he ever had in the twenty years since he'd quit. I'm glad he didn't.

I think my sister must have got hold of Alan, because at that point, he came into the casualty unit too. He was working as a builder. He was still covered in plaster from his day at work. He was shocked at the sight of me. My dad gently explained what had happened to me and what the doctor had said. Alan later said that he immediately imagined the worst outcomes imaginable, wheelchairs, brain damage, persistent vegetive state, death...

My dad asked Alan if he knew why I was going to Daytona as it was my day off, and Dad knew that I had other things to do at home too. Alan explained that I had gone there to collect some money that I was owed by a friend. At that point my mum came back in from her cigarette. Dad and Alan didn't tell her why I had gone out, they thought there was enough on her plate as it was and didn't want to upset her further.

I was moved to the intensive care unit in the hospital, freeing up much needed space in the casualty unit. My parents were exhausted, neither had eaten since breakfast time and they'd been to sick with worry to even think about food during the day. Alan volunteered to spend the night in the hospital with me, and promised to call if there was any change. Mum and Dad kissed me goodbye and quietly entreated me to wake up. I remained unconscious and they left.

Later I learned that Alan had sat by my bed all night. He sat there and talked to me about our holidays, motorbikes and adventures through the years. This was the best thing he could do. I would have been unconsciously aware of him, and that could help me to come round.

Alan has always had a stubborn streak, and this kept him going throughout the night. When my parents arrived the next morning the nursing staff explained that my "brother" hadn't left my side, even for a drink or to use the toilet as he hadn't wanted to leave me alone. Mum and Dad explained that although we weren't brothers by blood, our close friendship was akin to being brothers.

My dad dragged Alan away for a cup of tea, before sending him home to get some rest. His eyes were bloodshot and he was exhausted. Alan still had his sense of humour intact - it was one of the things I have always liked about him - and turned to where I lay and said "Suppose you want a cuppa..."

Mum sat by the bed, and as she talked to me, she noticed me twitch slightly. She called the nurse over to say that I had moved. The nurse explained that this was my brain's way of establishing connections with different parts of my body, discovering which nerves still worked. This was seen as a very good sign so soon after the actual accident. The nurse then telephoned someone to report this. It was not long after that Dad and Alan returned to the ward and Mum told them that I'd twitched. Alan said the minor twitches he'd seen me make were what had spurred him to keep talking all night long.

Shortly afterwards, two medical staff arrived, a doctor and a professor; the professor turned out to be one of the leading brain specialists in Europe, a man called Professor Rushton. My parents were reassured by the presence of the professor as it demonstrated just how seriously my case was being taken by the hospital. The professor explained that I was to have another MRI scan to see if there had been any change in my brain's condition and swelling.

Chapter Six

My brain had stopped swelling. It remained swollen, but at least it wasn't getting worse. My parents and Alan were finally told the extent of my injuries. My brain had taken the full force of decelerating from thirty miles per hour to a standstill in a split second, causing the frontal lobes to bang into the front of my skull. That impact was what had caused the initial swelling. My brain had rattled around inside my skull, like a pea in a whistle. Although the inside of the skull has some sharp protrusions, thankfully none had penetrated the brain itself. It had rubbed against the sides of my skull though, scuffing the areas that dealt with emotion. At this point Professor Rushton paused before saying "Kevin will be quite different when he wakes up".

My family were more interested in when I would wake up, but the professor explained he couldn't say, but that the longer I slept the better as it gave the brain more time to recover.

Nan, ever the matriarch, had decreed that she would visit me in hospital and if my dad didn't pick her up, she would get the bus. This was no idle threat, and to ensure my dual walking-stick wielding grandmother didn't carry out her threat, Dad and Alan got in the cab and went to pick her up. As Dad drove back to the hospital, Alan suggested that we get the traditional hospital gift for me; a bunch of grapes in case I woke up and was hungry.

They arrived back at the ward. Nan had been fully briefed by Dad and Alan on my condition, she made a beeline for my bed and say down next to me, talking to me. Her words rang round the ward, but were unheeded by me. I just lay there unconscious and unresponsive.

I lay there, still and unmoving as family and friends came to visit and talk to me. Doctors carried out various tests, but could give my family no further information about when I might possibly wake or how I would be. This was my second day of unconsciousness and the doctors said that this had moved me into a different category of head injury. Because I had been unconscious for more than twenty-four hours, I was now categorised as 'severe traumatic brain injury'. The statistics that go with this classification are sobering. My future life could be seriously impaired; of the six thousand, seven hundred and fifty people in the UK[1] who receive a severe traumatic brain injury annually, sixty per cent never return to work. Thankfully, my parents were not made aware of that fact at the time. They would have been even more worried about my future.

www.headway.org.uk/facts.aspx

Alan took the week off work, he stayed with me every night, just talking to me or watching films on my hospital television. He knew why I had made that trip to Daytona to collect the money, and felt that he should challenge my friend about it. He'd put off returning the money a couple of times and Alan felt that he shouldn't put off repaying the money once more. But at the same time, he didn't want to worry my parents about it and put any further strain on them. So he just sat with me and talked.

During the day, my parents would visit and Alan would stay until lunchtime to spend some time with them and update them about my status. My parents and Alan would normally have lunch together and this would give the nurses time to wash me and change the bed linens. This day, Nan had come along with Mum and Dad. She and Alan talked about the snooker championships. My nan was convinced that the modern players were unprofessional and that it had been better in her day.

They finished lunch and returned to the ward, ready to sit down and talk to me as the nurses would have finished washing me. The curtains around my bed were still pulled closed and some nurses nearby were talking about me. The fear that I had died while they had lunch gripped them, Mum and Dad ran across to my bed and pulled the curtains open. Four doctors were talking to me and my eyes were open. I was alive!

My parents started to say everything that had wanted me to hear since the accident, but I did not respond. A nurse ran over to ask them to step away, to give the doctors room to work. She also explained that although I had woken up, I hadn't moved. The thoughts of paralysis and brain damage ran through my parents' minds.

The intensive care unit of any hospital is a busy place, and my parents had to wait outside the ward while the doctors finished their tests. My parents had never been so glad about the creation of mobile phones. They took the time to make some calls to friends and family to tell them that I had finally woken up. My nan was convinced that God and my late grandfather were watching over me, her faith in them never wavering.

After what must have seemed like the longest time ever, but what in reality must have been no more than a few minutes, a nurse came to speak to them. She explained that a doctor would speak to them before they could see me. A few moments passed and then the doctor arrived.

"Kevin is conscious, he came around two minutes ago," she stated, looking relieved, "but he cannot register anything on his left hand side. This will change, it's just that the brain is still severely swollen."

"Can we see him?" asked Mum.

"Yes, please only stay for a minute though," came the reply, "he needs his rest."

To reduce the number of people at my bedside and avoid overstimulating me, Alan and my nan stayed back to let my parents spend a minute with me. Mum and Dad walked to the right-hand side of the bed. I was sitting propped up and looking forwards with a blank gaze, like a day-dreamer. My eyelids began to droop, but mum moved and my eyes flicked towards her and Dad. Dad moved a bit closer and my eyes tracked his movement before I fell asleep. Later, Mum said that my gaze was like a "dead man's stare".

As they moved away from my bed, a nurse approached them and asked to have a quiet word. She explained that because I had regained consciousness, I would be moved from intensive care to the high dependency unit. Mum and Dad were relieved as it was the next step in my recovery. They thanked the nurse, and then went to update Nan and Alan.

My sister Jenny lived next door to us, with her two daughters Montana and Savannah. As Dad pulled the cab onto the drive, Montana ran outside shouting "Uncle's awake isn't he?" They could hear my sister shouting Montana, calling her indoors knowing full well that Mum and Dad would be over with more details when they were ready.

My parents, Nan and Alan trooped indoors for a cup of tea. Nan looked at my mum and asked "What's wrong? You've been very quiet since we left hospital. What was the boy like?" Mum knew that Nan was hinting at me being brain damaged, but couldn't acknowledge it. She just said "I thought we lost him." Nan just hugged Mum close and for the first time since my accident, Mum allowed herself the time to cry.

Alan finished his drink and took his leave. He needed to let his parents know what had happened, and I think he realised that close as he was to us all, my family just needed some time together.

Mum, Dad and Nan sat up late into the night discussing what they knew about the accident, pieces they'd gleaned from police and doctors. They couldn't understand how I'd been so severely injured but had no real visible wounds or bruises. After numerous cups of tea and hours of talking, Dad drove Nan home. When he got back home, he and Mum spoke some more. My mum was terrified that I hadn't recognised her and wondered if I ever would. All my dad could say was to take each day at a time.

The next morning was a bright one. Mum and Dad heard the dustmen's van outside and Auzzie's distinctive voice yelling at my sister "Tell Kevin to hurry up and get out!" Subtlety had never been his strong point, but hearing that made my parents laugh, something they hadn't done in over a week.

Once again, my parents made their way to the hospital in Dad's cab. My mum nervously chain-smoked for the entire trip. She was still worried in case I had forgotten who she was. Dad focused on how supportive the rest of the family and their friends had been. Although the route to the hospital was a familiar one, this time their final destination was different. I had been judged well enough to leave intensive care for the high dependency unit.

Chapter Seven

My parents were greeted by a familiar face. One of the nurses was a friend; Alan's neighbour Monique. She greeted my parents, "Hello," she smiled kindly, "don't worry, we'll look after Kevin. And I'll try and get him onto a side ward." Her words eased some of my parents' concerns and fears, but not all of them. But at least they knew I would receive excellent care from someone who knew me.

The ward looked like it had been transplanted from the geriatrics unit, and I looked out of place, a child among senior citizens. I lay there, once again propped up and gazing blankly ahead.

"Hello Kevin," my father spoke quietly, not wanting to disturb the peace of the ward, "me and your mum are here." There was a short pause while my brain processed the words. I looked at Dad and then returned to gazing blankly at nothing. The tea lady came by at that moment and asked if I wanted some tea. Her words sounded like gibberish to me and I just looked at her. Mum answered for me "Yes please, only half a cup." I looked at Mum but said nothing.

Dad tried to get me talking, asking me questions about how I'd slept and if I wanted my tea. He knew any answers would take their time in coming. I glanced around, and ignoring his questions asked "Where am I?" before starting to cry. Mum just gathered me in her arms to cuddle and hold me while I wept. At first I pulled away, but then cuddled back down, the safety of her arms calming me. Again I asked where I was, and when Mum told me I was in hospital I just stared at her, still not really knowing who she was.

A new doctor appeared and asked to speak to my parents privately. The walked to one side and the doctor explained that the brain injuries would mean I was a changed person and would have trouble with my memory. He also explained that he would ask me some questions and monitor my responses. They then returned to my bedside.

"Good morning Kevin, how was your night?" I gave the doctor the same blank look that I gave everyone else. He tried to explain about the accident to me and explained that I'd injured my brain. I must have understood some of it, as I reached for my father and sobbed into his arms.

The doctor asked me if I knew how old I was and where I was. I responded that I was fifteen and in Africa. The doctor noted my responses, thanked me and walked away. Dad tried to explain to me that I was twenty-two and in London. Then once an hour, a nurse would come and ask me the same questions. My replies varied, but my age was always thirteen to fifteen years old. My location changed too. One hour I'd be in Jamaica, then Spain or China. My dad asked me why I thought I was in these different countries, and I'd point to the nurses with different ethnicities and nationalities.

I'd been born and raised in Peckham which is a very multi-cultural area, a real melting pot of races. There were no Mediterranean looking nurses on the ward, so the doctors thought my referencing Spain could be a small memory of wanting to move there.

Alan came to visit me, at first I didn't know who he was, but then I remembered him and our friendship. I think this hurt Mum as I still hadn't really recognised her. She'd read accounts of people with amnesia not knowing their own children or spouses and feared that I wouldn't ever remember her.

Looking back, I am very glad that both Mum and Dad had the support of not only family, but friends too. Alan's parents, Steve and Terry, would visit me in hospital, not that I really noticed them much at the time! Terry would spend time with Mum, sharing her fears and worries as only another mother can. They'd stand together outside, talking and smoking with the ever-present ambulance sirens wailing in the background. Terry had been with Alan as he cried about me, and now she did the same for Mum. Mum had been given worrying statistics by doctors and was scared for my future. Only forty per cent of people with severe traumatic brain injuries ever returned to work, and the majority of them were unable to work full-time. Terry reminded her that I was young and strong, which gave me a better chance and said that Alan would nag me better as he still needed a partner to hit the bars and clubs with. Little things like that made Mum smile.

My recovery was slow and little things I did were seen as huge steps. I spent most of my time in hospital sitting propped up in bed, not really interacting with the world or people around me. The first time I asked to walk to the toilets rather than have the nurse attend to me in bed was seen as a major breakthrough, especially as I asked Alan to walk me there. After that I would make my own way there, holding onto the drip stand, and head to the ward toilet.

I still don't know why, but one night I decided I wanted to use the toilet just off the corridor rather than the one on the ward. I made my way out to the corridor and looked around me. I didn't know where I was or how to get back to me bed. I walked to the nurses' station, confused and bleary. I was talking nonsense and crying, jumbling up needing the toilet with escape routes and being lost. I started crying for my mother.

No one with a relative in hospital wants the telephone to ring at quarter to three in the morning; it is invariably a harbinger of bad news. My mum answered the call, fearing the worst. The poor nurse on night duty was requesting that my parents get to the hospital as soon as possible, as I was crying hysterically for my mother and was refusing to move from the corridor until Mum was there. The other patients may not have appreciated my racket, but for my mum, to know that I had asked for her, remembered her, this was her gift; her baby was back.

My parents rushed to the hospital, and when I caught sight of Mum I actually jumped up to cuddle her, my crying stopped and Mum took me back to bed. This is one of the few things I remember from this time, I remember the safety and warmth of being in her arms, being held close and comforted back to sleep.

Over the next few days my memory started improving. I remembered being in Camberwell, and more parts of my life. However, the emotional turmoil caused by the brain injury meant that this manifested in tears. I would just sit there crying. This was very difficult for my family to deal with, but as the doctors explained to my parents, there were deep gouges along the side of my brain, and as I healed, my brain would have to find new ways to route the neural impulses that controlled emotions and I'd be more emotional as the brain rewired itself and could misinterpret emotions. It was a long-winded way of saying that I'd spend a lot of time crying even when I wanted to laugh or smile. But it meant that I was healing.

When my parents visited, I was able to greet them and even better, knew who they were. My mum would get a little bit teary, this would set me off and then Dad's defenses would fail and we'd all hug and hold each other crying. We got through a lot of tissues.

When the doctors came in to check on me, I would try to read what was on the back of my medical notes. Mum later said that it reminded her of when I was young and would read the back pages of Dad's newspaper. I wouldn't really understand what I was reading, but just enjoyed the action of reading.

As my memory continued improving, I had another MRI scan. It was a routine procedure for me now, even though I was unhappy at leaving my parents behind. This would enable the doctors to see how badly my brain was damaged, hopefully without the previous swelling in the way.

While we waited for the results, I sat by the window in the ward, looking out at the view. I mentioned that it reminded me of looking out of the window during my business studies classes at school. My parents kept quiet, knowing that allowing me the space and time access my memories was the best thing they could do.

Thirty minutes later my results were ready. One of the doctors arrived and with him was the same professor who had been there when I was initially admitted into hospital. I later thought he looked a little like Sir Isaac Newton, the great mathematician. He greeted my parents and said hello to me. I didn't reply, I was off in my own little world again. He explained to my parents that the swelling around my frontal lobes had decreased significantly and that he felt I was now ready to be moved to the recovery and rehabilitation centre. It was just over the road from the hospital and called Mapother House. I was to be moved there the very next day.

Chapter Eight

The next day came and started normally. I ate some cereal for breakfast, looked out of the window and cried at nothing. My mum arrived, and this time there was an unfamiliar man with her. I looked at him and then I remembered him. It was Marcus, a friend from work. That was enough for the tears to start again. Marcus had been warned that I was emotional and cried a lot, but I think he was overwhelmed by how bad I was. He found it difficult and upsetting to look at me, but he sat there and talked to me.

A porter arrived to move me across to Mapother House. Marcus steered my wheelchair, him still talking and me still crying, the porter bringing my personal belongings. I remembered Marcus and some of our history together, but couldn't stop crying long enough to tell him that. Marcus continued telling me about colleagues and customers, but this just set me off again, crying even harder than before. Mum had to soothe and calm me down. This was too much for Marcus to deal and cope with, so he decided to leave.

Mum thanked Marcus for visiting and helping with the move, she explained again that my crying was a good sign of my memories returning, but understood how difficult it was to see.

My new 'home' was a six-bed ward, and I was the youngest person in it. Mapother House usually handled rehabilitation for older patients who'd suffered strokes, not young bikers who'd come off worst against lorries. The bed to my left contained an older man called Lloyd, he made a movement that signaled a greeting. I didn't know what to do, so I looked at Mum.

"Say hello Kevin, this is Lloyd," she'd seen his name on the small board by his bed.

"Hello," I obediently said, following Mum's instructions. I didn't really know what else to do

At that point, my dad arrived. He'd been taking Nan to the optician. It was a reminder that even though I was still injured, other people's lives continued and they still had chores and errands to run. Lloyd made a movement again, this time towards a list on his bed. It was the lunch list. Dad picked it up for him, Lloyd would depend on people to help him after his stroke. I think he could tell my dad was uneasy about me being in the ward and this was his way of easing my dad's mind about my care.

Mum and me watched while Dad went through the lunch options with Lloyd. When Dad read out the option he wanted, Lloyd would grunt his choice. I think Lloyd knew what was on the menu, but this was his way of breaking the ice with us.

The catering nurse came round and introduced herself. She was a jolly woman and her friendly manner made me feel accepted. This was a great feeling to have, but it overwhelmed me and once more, I burst into tears. Mum ordered my lunch for me...

Time passed in Mapother House, my parents would talk about my past or just what was happening at home. I started remembering more about my life. Sometimes I would comment, sometimes I'd still stare blankly at nothing and sometimes I'd cry. During my early days there, Lloyd watched me cry for hours. Eventually Lloyd left for home and I missed him. But that was the aim of Mapother, to get you ready for life at home. Lloyd would never be fully independent and need people to help him, but at least he was at home.

I saw different specialists, they all helped me in different ways, even the ones I disagreed with. I may have had a brain injury, but I was well enough to argue. I was getting better and my old personality was slowly coming back.

Soon enough, a new patient was admitted and he took Lloyd's old bed. He was a Turkish man whose name I don't recall. He had also suffered a stroke, this had affected the part of his brain that deals with behaviour. He was a grown man acting like a naughty schoolchild, smoking on the ward and playing pranks. It may have been funny for us, but not quite so funny for the nursing staff!

As I continued improving, I spent more time out of bed and in the T.V. room. We would go there to eat, watch telly and just get out of the ward while the nurses changed the sheets or we just wanted a change of scenery. The T.V room opened out to a garden area where the smokers would go for a nicotine fix. In those early days, I didn't remember that I was a smoker, but that changed as my memory returned.

Reality and the perception of reality are two entirely different things. In reality, I was in a rehab ward recovering from a very severe brain injury. In my perception of reality, I was in a coma and this was all just a dream and I needed to escape from Mapother House. Needless to say, the specialists I was seeing all said this was not the case, that I was awake and really in rehab. I didn't believe them. In fact, as the days progressed, I became more and more convinced that my dream theory was fact and that to escape I needed to lie and tell the specialists what they wanted to hear.

One night a familiar face came to see me. It was Craig, my boss from Daytona. Out of everyone who'd visited me, he took my condition the worst. Either that or everyone else had been really good at hiding their reactions. He had been warned that I would cry, and I did. He sat there talking to me and I sat there crying. He knew that talking and crying were essential for my recovery but that didn't make it easier for him to see. I think he had trouble reconciling the crying wreck before him with the cocky young mechanic in his mind. When he left, he didn't look back. I don't think he wanted me to see him crying.

It wasn't long before I was moved from the six-bed ward to a smaller three-bed one. There were two other occupants, a sleeping man whose name I forget and another man recovering from a stroke. He was called Tom and had been left partially disabled from it. He seemed like a nice man. The sleeping man soon left the ward and was replaced by a young man called Islam. He was only twenty-three and an unlikely candidate for a stroke. He was young and healthy, he wasn't overweight, he didn't drink or smoke and ate reasonably healthy food. Nonetheless, here he was in stroke rehab.

I would try to keep myself busy and my mind active. I read the magazines that were left lying around the ward and T.V room, and I even tried reading a book from the library, but started drift off mid-page. Mind you, I was like that with books before the accident! Another thing I liked doing was being Tom's legs. He had lost his mobility with his stroke and was getting used to maneuvering his new wheelchair around, but he still wasn't really up to being out of bed for long, so I would run around getting him cups of tea. I'm still not sure if Tom actually wanted as much tea as I brought him, but he could see that I enjoyed being useful and helping!

Every night my parents would visit and Dad would always leave the newspaper with me. Reading it at night always helped me fall asleep. Over time, my cigarette habit came back and I would occasionally pop out for a cheeky smoke.

One night, my mum could not visit me as she had some essential chores to do at home - it was good to think that I was well enough for her to get on with doing the other things she needed to do. I telephoned my dad and asked him to bring me one of my favourite meals, a large doner kebab with extra chili sauce. That was another thing I had loved before the accident and another sign that I was becoming me again. Dad brought the kebab with him and I shared it with Islam, there are few finer meals than a decent doner!

Time passed by at Mapother House. The whole point of being there was to prepare me for life in the real world and to help acclimatise me to it, I was allowed to spend weekends at home. I would go home, watch telly and spend time with the people I love. My parents were thrilled that I was well enough for these weekend visits, but I don't think that my dad was so thrilled whenever his twenty-two year old baby had a nightmare and ended up sleeping in the bed he shared with Mum and Dad ended up on the sofa! In my defense, sleeping in my own room brought back so many memories that my brain had problems processing them all and this manifested as nightmares that only Mum could keep me safe from.

Before the accident, I would play GP500 online. My favourite track was the Jerez track in Spain and I had decided that I would actually ride there once I moved to Spain. One Sunday at home, the Moto GP was on telly and it was at Jerez. I really enjoyed watching the race, I think it linked to the memories of heading to Spain and it was just one of those really nice things I remember from then.

I would spend the weekends at home, and come Sunday evening I would get all my things together to return to Mapother House with. Mondays were when I would see a variety of therapists and specialists and clash with them about my dream theory. I ended up thinking that I would have to just agree with them just to get out of there!

When a person is in a coma, they often don't come out of it as soon as people would like because they are inhabiting a dream world they don't want to leave. I was convinced that I was in such a dream state and starting to rebel against it and wake up. So I continued with the therapy, home visits and even assisted work experience - all the time believing it was all a dream.

To aid with my rehabilitation I started working back at Daytona for two days a week. I'd get the bus there with my occupational health therapist, and then she'd supervise me in the workplace. I think the organised chaos of my workplace shocked my therapist but for me, it was good to be back with friends. My first day back there was very emotional for me, a few customers who I'd grown pally with came in to see me and as usual, I got tearful. This was difficult for people to deal with, but people would back off a bit to give me space to compose myself.

I suffered from occasional panic attacks, one of these happened on the journey to work, and I had to get off the bus. I ended up handling the situation and coping well with the attack before continuing my journey to work.

I was staying at home for weekends and working supervised for two days a week. I was still convinced that this was just a dream, but kept that idea to myself. I didn't want the therapists and doctors to delay my full release, agreeing with them was the only way for me to leave Mapother House and wake up.

Chapter Nine

Finally I was able to leave Mapother House and return home. I had shed a few tears as I said goodbye to people I had become really close to, including Tom. I think he was relieved that he wouldn't be forced to drink so much tea! We exchanged phone numbers and said we'd keep in touch.

My dad arrived to pick me up, he had a beaming great smile on his face, he was so happy that I had recovered enough to come home. He had become a familiar face on the ward, so joined in on the goodbyes. The other patients had grown to really like him, in part because of his generous and kind nature. Nothing was ever too much trouble as far as he was concerned.

As I left Mapother House, my heart raced with the excitement of going home. It was like that feeling you get when you're nearly home after a holiday and you just want comfy, familiar surroundings. As we drove home, memories associated with the area started flooding back, the times spent hanging out on street corners with Alan and other friends, the places we'd visit and the newsagents where we'd buy sweets. Dad pulled the cab over and stopped at that newsagents to buy a paper for me to read later on.

We got home and Dad drove the cab up onto the driveway, my niece Montana was waiting in the front garden next door. She ran over and hugged me. Yes, it was good to be home!

I vaguely remembered Jenny and the girls visiting me, but the early days after the accident were a blur, like a half-remembered dream. My sister was very relieved to see me out of hospital, but she understood that I wasn't the same Kevin as before.

Walking into the house, I was glad to see that it looked familiar. I carried my bag upstairs and went to my bedroom. I went to the bedroom I'd had when I was thirteen years old, not the room I inhabited as an adult. My brain had almost got stuck at me being thirteen, and even though I remembered pieces past that, it did seem to be almost a default setting.

Walking into the correct bedroom, I saw all my posters and pictures on the walls. I remembered sitting in there playing my Spanish language CDs and online motorbike racing. The pictures were of friends, family and motorbikes, days out, holidays and parties. I had always loved having visual reminders of good times, so the memories were always there. Maybe I'd somehow known I'd need the help in the future? But here was my life in photos. Once more I was overwhelmed by an emotional tidal wave of memories, and once more I was crying, this time in the bathroom.

Dad heard the sound of me sobbing, he knocked on the bathroom door and asked if I was alright. I sobbed out that everything was too much; my poor dad was not well-equipped to deal with over-emotional sons. He said he'd get Mum. Dad stayed with me until Mum arrived home from work. I could see how upset my dad was. It was strange to see such a normally happy man so sad. And not for the last time, Mum held and comforted me while I cried myself to sleep.

My short-term memory was still patchy. One of my first visitors was Auzzie. We sat and chatted for an hour and it was good to be with a friend, but after he left I could not for the life of me remember what we had spoken about. I had to start following the advice I got in Mapother House and start making notes!

The longer I spent at home, among my family, friends and belongings, the less I believed that life was a coma-dream and gradually accepted that this was my life and that it was real. At varying times of day, I would still get upset and cry. Whoever was with me would calm me down and let me cry myself out. It wasn't easy for my family and friends to deal with, but it was a sign that my brain was forging new pathways and healing. The hospital had advised me to not push myself too hard and not to be too hard on myself, but I was impatient and felt that because I was at home that I should be better. I was still working part-time hours at Daytona. I gradually increased my hours to three days a week, thinking that I could handle my emotions. I was wrong.

I had always been a happy-go-lucky sort of chap, and despair had always been a foreign feeling to me. So when out of the blue, dark suicidal thoughts struck, I was not best equipped to deal with them. I was sitting on the bus, going to work and as the bus travelled over Blackfriars Bridge across the Thames, a panic attack hit me. Then my thoughts got more scary as I realised that I could fill my pockets with rocks and swim down to the bottom of the river. The rocks would hold me down. I managed to fight the feelings and continued on my way to work. The feelings would return and sometimes overwhelmed me. One day at work, a princess saved my life.

Andy AKA Princess was working with me and saw my mood darken over the course of the day. To distract me, he offered me a cigarette, my smoking habit having firmly been re-established. As we sat and smoked, I started talking. I was so open and honest with him, he was better than any therapist and I told Princess about my despair, my bleakness and my suicidal moments. He listened to everything I said without judging me. That was an amazing feeling of friendship.

After I had poured my heart out, Princess look at me, his long hair tied back out of the way from machinery and stray sparks. He told me about his brother, who had been injured in an accident similar to mine and had similar injuries and how he'd coped. At first I thought that Princess had invented a fictional brother as a way to get through to me, but as he continued his tale and his pain was evident, I believed him.

Over the next few months, these feelings would come more regularly. One day I was watching a video about disability and brain injuries, made by a company called HeadWay. It featured a man who had physical disabilities after a brain injury, and before I knew it I was sitting there arguing with myself about how much worse my situation was. People make allowances for people with visible disabilities, they can see that there is something wrong. Me, I had a brain injury that changed everything about me and no one could tell just by looking at me. No one would make any allowance for me. These thoughts swirled round my mind and added to my depressive moments.

I told Mum about these emotions; thankfully she took this in her stride too, not over-reacting or panicking. Her stock answer to me was "It would be a great loss to lose you after everything you've been through". One day she was even blunter with me, saying that if I did kill myself "It would end Nan." That did stop me in my tracks, there was no way I would ever want do anything to hurt my beloved grandmother.

Chapter Ten

One week after leaving Mapother House for the final time, I started full time work back at Daytona. There was a worry from doctors and family that I was pushing myself too quickly, but I wanted to stay busy. I found that too much time to myself meant that I would get the low moods that plagued me.

To defeat the panic attacks that hit me on the bus, Mum suggested I get a portable CD player. The music stopped my mind from roaming to dark places. For a couple of months my life revolved around work, commuting and home. I would sit in my room and listen to music, my favourite tracks playing over and over again. One Friday night, I logged onto the online racing game GP500 that I had played almost religiously before the accident.

I was instantly among familiar names and was bombarded with questions about how the move to Spain had gone, why I hadn't been in touch with people and when could I meet a player in Barcelona for a beer. I posted a long message on the main page about what had happened and my recovery. For a minute or so, there was silence from all the players as they read my post, then one of my oldest online friends, his online handle was Dolz, suggested we race at Jerez. It was my favourite track and he knew that. It was a really touching gesture and before I knew it, fifteen of us were lined up on Jerez's starting line.

The lights went green and we all pulled away and I quickly slotted into second place behind Dolz. Corners sped past, my competitive streak emerged and despite taking a few corners quite wide, it wasn't long before I was in the lead. It was at that point that the penny dropped, they were letting me win. It was a lovely intention, but it wasn't how I wanted to race. I wanted to win properly. My attempt to set a new lap record was thwarted when I realised I couldn't remember where the brake markers were.

I won the race, but as it was fixed, it didn't feel like a win. I thanked the online guys, but I had decided to leave the GP500 forum so wanted to say goodbye. It may seem silly, but I felt sad at leaving these people who I had never actually met but still had experienced great times with.

My driving licence had been, unsurprisingly, revoked and I didn't want to travel on the bus if I didn't have to. I would sit indoors and watch the world go by, or watch telly or listen to music. Occasionally I would go and see Alan, but his family business meant that he worked long hours and was often busy. However, despite that, he did find the time to spend with me.

I had been back at home for two or three months, when Alan and me decided to go out, like we would before the accident. We took his mum's car, we were dressed up, looking pretty smart and headed to the nightspots of Guildford. At first I was a bit scared, it was my first night out since the accident and I didn't know how I would react in the crowded pubs and bars.

We walked around the area, After a couple of hours I was ready to go home. It was all a little bit overwhelming for me, but I was happy and had had a nice time, but a couple of hours was enough for my first night out!

Alan made sure to take me out every so often and ensured I didn't become a recluse, living in my room, playing online, watching DVDs of me racing at Brands Hatch, moping and listening to music.

One evening I was sitting there having had yet another low moment, when some advice given to me by the psychologist at Mapother House sprang to mind, "Try using Friends Reunited to meet old school friends to help your memory". He said that talking to old friends would help me regain some of my lost memories, and that he was sure people would want to help me.

In today's world, social and professional networks like Facebook, Twitter and LinkedIn are central to many peoples' lives. They are a free service and we update them from our phones and tablets, telling our friends about our thoughts, dreams and plans, as well as sharing funny pictures, mainly of cats it seems! Back in the early 2000s, social networking was in its infancy and Friends Reunited led the field with its subscription-based service.

I created a free account, logged in and searched for my old school. The psychologist was right, seeing all those names that I had forgotten did spark some memories. I sat back and started reminiscing about things, some funny, some sad, but memories nonetheless. I wanted to get in contact with some of the people, but was too scared to make that first step.

As I was looking on the list of schools near my school, I noticed there was a nearby girls' school listed. It was called Waverley Girls' School and for some reason, I was drawn to the name. I didn't know why the school name drew me in, but it was like when someone says not to look at something, so you want to look at it. So I looked at it.

I looked at the names for my school year and a few names jumped out at me, jogging memories of my local estate and hanging out with the other kids at weekends and in holidays. Before I left the school site, I decided to have a quick look at the years above and below me. Again, I recognised a couple of names and then suddenly, BANG!

My head was reeling with the intensity of the memories. Jane Peart. My former girlfriend, the first love of my life and here she was on Friends Reunited. My brain swam with the memories, hanging round Surrey Quays, the kisses, the fun and the good times. Before I knew it, fifteen minutes had passed in a daydreaming haze. The memories of Jane triggered more memories and the soundtrack of that summer played in my head; Chaka Demus and Pliers jostling for space with Dina Carroll.

Having a reminisce sounds quite nice, but when you have suffered memory loss and a brain injury, the flood of memories just swarming into your conscious mind is overwhelming. It is also physically tiring and draining sorting those memories out, arranging them into a chronological order and understanding where in your personal timeline they fit. It also renders you pretty useless at work the next day...

Saturdays at Daytona usually meant that Princess would tell me what he and his girlfriend had been up to, and then if it was quiet enough, eat pizza. This Saturday, my mind was back in the 1990s. Princess could see that I was distracted and let me talk about things. I was mainly concerned with Jane Peart and where she might be now. It does seem odd, focusing on a girl that I had gone out with and then dumped when we were in our early teens, but that is where my mind was.

Normally, at the end of the day, I would put my headphones on and walk to the bus stop and watch all my workmates ride away on their motorbikes. I loved watching that, my love of motorbikes was still strong despite the accident.

Today though, I walked away, listening to a recording of the Leeds Festival 2000 and wondering how I would word my profile on Friends Reunited. My psychologist had said it be therapeutic, so who was I to ignore such good advice?

Once home I went up to my room, sat in front of my computer and lit another cigarette. I upgraded my free Friends Reunited account to a paying member account; this allowed me to message other people on the site and talk to them. I wrote a brief profile for my account and then sat back and started worrying. I really wanted to message Jane, but would she want to talk to me? Was she in a relationship or married? Did she have kids? What should I say to her?

My mind was swirling and my emotions were all over the place. I was scared and nervous but I started typing out a message to her. The message took a lot of attempts to write, I didn't want to sound scary or fake or creepy, so I kept rewriting it until it sounded right. Eventually, I took a deep breath and hit send.

It took a couple of days for Jane to reply to me. While waiting for her reply, I imagined all the different responses she could send from "yeah great - let's get together" to the "Go away - you broke my heart" and everything in between. I was nervous and excited and finally she replied. She was sorry to hear about the accident, but didn't really think she could be of any help to me. I started to cry, I felt that what could have been a strong source of help had been taken away from me. I felt alone and scared, but finished reading the message. Towards the end of the message she had added "If I can help, I would like to. Here is my number."

My heart was racing, I was crying and my breathing sped up. For a moment I couldn't tell if it was a heart attack or panic attack. For some reason then, Jane scared me. I think it was the intensity of the emotions and memories that were hitting me. I remembered getting drunk in the mid 1990s; wishing I hadn't dumped her and wanting to get back together with her, I remembered her smile from when we did go out. As I cried myself out, my heart rate slowed down, and the sick feeling in my guts left. I sat back and chain-smoked four cigarettes before going back to the computer to re-read her message. The sick feeling came back, but I forced myself to sit there and note down Jane's phone number.

As I looked at the number written down on a piece of paper, I realised that I remembered it. It was Jane's home phone number. I decided to phone her and ask to meet up, partially to help my memory and partially because it felt right to see Jane after ten years had passed.

I decided to plan the conversation as I didn't want to give the wrong impression and just babble at her or worse, just be lost for words. I had a gut feeling that this could be a life changing moment and I didn't want to ruin it. I wrote down what I wanted to say, picked up the receiver and dialed.

A woman answered the phone on the third ring. I wasn't sure if it was Jane or not, so I asked if Jane was there. The woman said she would get her, so I waited. After a short pause, a voice said "Hello?". It was Jane. I said hello and said that it was Kevin who had messaged her on Friends Reunited. I quickly explained about the accident and my injuries and their effects. When I stopped talking, there was an uncomfortable pause as I realised that I had just bombarded Jane with all my problems. So much for my planned conversation, I must have sounded crazy. Then Jane spoke, "I'm sorry, but I am on my way out. I will email you." It was as if she had just hung up on me.

I walked back to my room. I was angry, I was hurt and upset. I was crying again. I didn't know what I'd expected from Jane, but I felt hurt. My room had become a safe space for me, I retreated into it, like a tortoise into its shell. But this time, I didn't feel safe in there. I was surrounded by pictures of the fun times, the motorbikes and everything that I enjoyed. I looked at the bike pictures, the pictures of the machines that I loved and the machines that had so dramatically altered my life. I felt cheated by them. If it wasn't for my love of motorbikes, I wouldn't have had that accident. I felt that depressive low feeling creep up on me, and I only thought about the worst possible outcomes for my life. I left my room and headed for the living room and Mum, hoping that she and the TV would distract me.

A line from a track called The End by The Doors echoed round my mind. Jim Morrison's voice singing "This is the end, My only friend the end" on constant replay, echoing in my mind. Then mid-chorus, the phone rang. Mum answered it and her side of the call sparked my interest. I had to get closer to overhear what was being said, but Mum was answering questions about me and the accident. At first I thought it was maybe a family member calling up for the latest news on me but Mum looked suspicious and worried, so it couldn't be family. Then as the call continued, Mum's expression changed and she was smirking slightly. The call ended and by then Mum was smiling.

Before I could even ask who it was, Mum explained that it was one of Jane's friends calling to see if my story of the accident and memory loss was true. As I smiled in relief, my mood lifted and I let out a huge breath of air I hadn't even realised I'd taken. I even felt ok about the excuse Jane had given during our conversation.

Later that evening, I received another message from Jane, she suggested that we meet up at the weekend. She said that she would pick me up and we could go for a meal. I think she was worried about my condition as she asked where I could go. I messaged back saying Blackheath and we agreed a time.

In a state of some excitement, I ran downstairs and told my parents that Jane had contacted me and that we were going for a meal in Blackheath. Mum quickly reminded me that Professor Rushton had said that I wasn't to drink alcohol and asked if Jane knew. I wasn't worried about not drinking alcohol. I was going to see Jane.

Chapter Eleven

I had become used to feelings of despondency and despair filling my mind, but the excitement of seeing Jane pushed them to one side. I was happy and everyone at work noticed the difference in me. I started talking to Princess, telling him what had happened. He was pleased to see me so happy and bouncy, but told me to be careful as I was not the person I used to be, and could be taken advantage of or used. I didn't think Jane would do that, but it was nice that he cared about me.

The week flew by and before I knew it, it was Saturday. Princess wished me luck and I ran to the bus stop, eager to get home and get ready for my evening out with Jane. As I sat on the bus, listening to music and idly watching the traffic, I thought about the times I could remember with Jane. I thought about splashing around in the docks, showing off while Jane and her friends watched.

I ran in through the front door and straight up the stairs. I yelled to Mum as I bolted upstairs "Gotta get ready! I'll be down soon!" I wanted to get showered and looking good for Jane. As I came back down, freshly showered and looking good, Mum asked me to come into the living room. I walked in and was worried because Mum looked worried. She looked at me, with concern in her eyes and said "I don't want you getting hurt. Be careful tonight, no drinking and don't make it late." I understood her concern as this was the first social outing I was going on since the accident without Alan and it was with someone who I hadn't seen in over a decade. I think that Mum had her own way, she would have driven me to Blackheath, waited outside the restaurant and driven me home again!

Jane had said that she would pick me up at seven o'clock. Seven o'clock came and went. My nerves were still fragile and I started to worry. Had Jane been in an accident or had she decided not to come. I kept calming myself down as I did not want to get stressed out at Jane if she turned up.

A car horn sounded at just past half past seven. I got up and walked to the door, Mum following behind me asking if I had my wallet and phone. My phone was still upstairs, so I rushed out to get it. Mum went out to the car to meet Jane and get a first impression of her. I don't know what was said, but I think Mum wanted to make sure that I would be safe that evening.

I stepped into the garden and took a long, deep breath. As I walked up to her car, Mum loudly (and mainly for Jane's benefit) repeated all she had said earlier about me not drinking alcohol and not staying out too late. And then, I saw her.

Jane was obviously older, but to my eyes she was even more beautiful. Her eyes were still the same startling green and her long chestnut brown curls brushed her shoulders. I got into the car and there were an awkward few moments and then we started making smalltalk, but we both wanted to talk about that past but didn't want to bombard and overwhelm each other. Jane started the car and as she reversed out of the driveway, I could see Mum, shadowy and distorted by the frosted glass of the front door, watching as we drove away.

The smalltalk and re-introductions had finished and there was a strained silence that lasted for a few minutes. Jane took the initiative and started talking about the past. I was struggling to take in everything that Jane was saying, I just listened out for questions and was able to answer some of them, like remembering Jane and her friend Natalie watching me and Gary play football. Even today, I don't fully remember all the conversation we had, but I think Jane might have sensed my difficulty in keeping up with her, as she suddenly asked me what I wanted to do in Blackheath. I said I just wanted to walk around for a bit.

In Blackheath, Jane pulled into the car park. We then walked into the village to look for somewhere to eat and talk. We found a small Italian restaurant and had the first of what would be many meals together. We sat and talked, only being quiet when the waiter arrived with our food. Jane quickly sensed that asking about my accident and exactly what I remembered made me uneasy, so she started talking about holidays she had been on, as well as the trip she was planning to Ayia Napa with her cousin. We compared notes and were surprised to see that we'd been to a lot of the same places, just not at the same time!

The conversation flowed and before I knew it, I was telling Jane about the trip to Spain that I'd planned. This lead onto the accident itself, and the extent of my injuries. Jane told me that I seemed fine, I don't know why, but this was comforting.

You know those quizzes or interview questions where you're asked to describe yourself as an animal? Well, I'd usually describe myself as a tortoise or turtle with a hard shell to protect and house me. It takes me a while to get used to people and open up to them. But talking with Jane was different. Before I knew it, we had been talking for two hours. A lot of the conversation had revolved around me and I wanted to know about Jane's life, so I suddenly asked her if she had a boyfriend. There was a moment of silence and I apologised for asking the question and my abruptness. Jane paused for a moment before explaining that she was in a relationship, but that it wasn't working out and she didn't know what to do.

I had a brain injury and may not have been the best person to the planet to give relationship advice. But I gave it anyway. I said that Jane should do what she feels would be best for her, or before she knows it, years will have gone by and she'd wonder where her life and the time had gone. I wasn't trying to get Jane to split up from this man, but genuinely just wanted her to be happy.

We shared the bill, I had wanted to pay it all, but Jane insisted on sharing and we left the restaurant heading back to the car. Jane had said that she would drive me home and we started the journey back. I still liked Jane, and I had thought about her and what she might be doing for years. To be blunt, I still fancied her and did not know how she felt about me. Did I have a chance with her? What about her boyfriend? How did she feel about me? Was I too much of a basket case? With all these thoughts swirling around my head, my brain reacted in the only way it knew to. I started to have a panic attack. Great.

Jane was talking to me and I was sitting there doing my best not to cry with emotional frustration. I couldn't even talk to her, I was too engrossed in not freaking out. Not that Jane knew this. All she could see was me, in the passenger seat, in a seemingly sullen silence. She gave up trying to hold a conversation with me and lapsed into an uncomfortable silence.

We pulled up to my parents' house and I literally leapt out of the car, a quick "Bye" muttered and I was gone, heading for the house and the security and safety of my bedroom. Poor Jane was left wondering what the blazes had happened and if anything she said had caused me to behave like that.

Mum and Dad had heard me rush in straight up, and were worried about me. I hadn't popped my head into the living room to say hello or anything, I'd just run straight upstairs. Dad was the first one to reach my room, and came straight over as he saw me sitting on my bed, crying and sobbing. He started asking me questions about what happened, but they all came out so thick and fast that I couldn't keep up. I just cuddled up to him and sobbed some more. By this time Mum had come in as well, and I was able to say that I'd had an amazing evening, but that I was having one of my "low moments" and would be downstairs shortly. Dad sensed that Mum was about to start playing twenty questions so he took her downstairs and let me calm myself down.

I sat on the bed and slowly collected my thoughts and calmed myself. It was a few minutes until I felt mentally strong enough to go downstairs and talk to Mum and Dad. We chatted about the evening, what me and Jane had spoken about and how I felt about her. There was even laughter about me still fancying Jane!

Dad sensibly advised that I should call Jane to let her know I was ok and that she hadn't upset me. I wanted to call straight away but didn't want to be a pest. So we sat there watching telly for an hour or so, before I picked up the phone. I explained that I hadn't wanted to be rude and that I was trying to control a panic attack. "You couldn't get out of the car fast enough, I was worried I'd said something wrong," Jane giggled before adding "I thought everything went well then you ran away with barely a goodbye." We chatted some more and agreed to meet up a few days later. I hoped that Jane wanted to spend more time with me, and as for me, it could trigger more memories of my past and I could be with Jane again. She made me feel, well, normal.

Chapter Twelve

Sunday started like most days. I would wake up upset and angry at the accident that had so drastically altered my life. Sometimes, especially in those early days, the upset would descend into a suicidal depression. Despite having had a nice evening (apart from the panic attack) with Jane, my mood spiraled down and I lay in bed crying. I made a decision. I decided to write a letter, a suicide letter that would explain everything.

Mum and Dad

I can't take it anymore, it has got the better of me, it is because of one person he was driving the lorry that day. I am sorry to be inconsiderate and take the easy option but I want it to stop in my head.

My nan, my friend, who has always been there for me, I can't explain this to anybody but you are the closest person who understands a bit. Some say it's the easy option but knowing the suffering I will leave, it's not.

Alan, my best mate, the times we shared were irreplaceable but I have won this competition bye.

Jane, what we could have been if we met sooner, thanks for your help.

Princess [Andy] without you, I would never have lived this long. Thanks for all the support at work, cheers.

Kevin

I sat there, I even made a plan of how I wanted my funeral to go, down to the colour clothes people wore. I wanted Alan in white, I wanted to make him realise how out of place I felt. It wasn't a nice thing to do, punishing him for how I felt, but my brain was not in a good place and I was lashing out.

So now all I had to do was to decide whether to actually kill myself, and I put it all on the toss of a coin. Heads I would die and tails I would live like a dog tail between the legs cowering. I held the coin in my hand, mentally saying all my goodbyes to everyone. Eventually, I had said my goodbyes and it was time to flip the coin.

Tails.

I had to live. Fate had decreed it through a coin toss. I couldn't stop having the suicidal thoughts, but I fought against them harder than ever. Sunday continued for me and I destroyed the suicide note. No one would ever have to read it, but the words stayed with me.

The next day I woke for work and felt a lot better, even happy in a way. Maybe it was because I was here, maybe it was my brain healing. I don't know, but my choice was made. I just had to get on with life now.

Life has a habit of moving on for everyone. I was learning to deal with the world again and changes were happening to my friends too. Some people at work were talking of leaving Daytona for jobs elsewhere and I knew that I would miss them.

Before the accident, I used to go on Sunday motorbike rides with Alan and Auzzie, either on my own bike or riding pillion with Auzzie. I missed that, the feeling of freedom and just enjoying the ride. But today was a major change for Auzzie. There was a ring at the door, as I opened the door, I saw Auzzie standing there. Instead of a "hello", the first words out of his mouth were "Kev, I've bought a car". I would have been less surprised if he'd said he was an alien in disguise! Auzzie lived and breathed motorbikes.

I invited Auzzie in and as we sat and chatted he told me that he'd had to give up riding on doctor's orders. Like many bikers, Auzzie had been in a few crashes over the years and had some broken bones along the way, especially in his legs. The doctor had been quite clear about one thing. If Auzzie broke his leg again there was a severe chance that it would not heal properly and that he could even lose the use of it.

I used to enjoy riding with Auzzie. Granted, he wasn't the quickest biker and sometimes got left behind, but I enjoyed riding with him. One of my favourite rides we'd shared were the Friday nights when we'd go to the bikers' meet on Chelsea Bridge. Auzzie in a car. I had honestly thought that day would never happen. But things and people change.

That week, emails and Friends Reunited messages flew between me and Jane. We agreed to meet up again that Friday and I couldn't wait. Friday evening arrived and I raced home to get changed. I think Mum was nearly as excited as me, it was good for her to see me feeling, well, so alive.

"With Jane is it?" she asked. My huge grin was all the answer she needed and Mum laughed as I flapped about, getting washed and changed. I was still upstairs getting ready when Jane pulled up outside and hooted the car horn for me. Mum went out and asked her to come in and wait while I finished getting ready. I was a bit concerned that Jane might feel pressured by that, but when I came downstairs she and Mum were chatting like old friends. It was really nice to see that, but I wanted to be on my own with Jane. Jane said goodbye to Mum and we left, heading for a new bar in Clapham.

It was a nice bar, although I think Jane was still a little uncomfortable because I still wasn't drinking alcohol. We found a quiet corner and chatted, and as we talked all I wanted to do was kiss Jane. I hoped that my eyes didn't betray my feelings as I didn't want to scare her off. If Jane didn't feel the same way as me, I would lose not only a potential girlfriend, but an actual friend.

We only stayed in the bar for one drink, Jane had suggested that we go for a drive. I liked the idea of that, I had always enjoyed just jumping on a bike or in a car and just heading off with no real destination in mind. The car radio was tuned to Kiss FM, a dance music station, and they played some club tracks I remembered from a few years ago. That naturally, made my emotions bubble up, and as I was keeping a lid on that, a group of about eight or so bikers overtook us, most likely heading for Chelsea Bridge. By this time I was mentally jumping on the lid of my emotions so that I wouldn't go to pieces in front of Jane. I think Jane sensed my struggle as she started talking to cover the silence.

We drove around for a bit longer, before heading back to my place. As we pulled up outside the house, we both said how much we'd enjoyed spending time together and we wanted to meet up again. I considered leaning over for a kiss, but wasn't sure what Jane's reaction would be. I sure as Hell didn't want to make the wrong move and destroy a friendship.

Over the few days, emails were exchanged and we met again. I realised that Jane wasn't just seeing me to help me regain my memories, as she could easily have been out having fun instead of helping with my rehabilitation. Our next date was on a moored river boat called Wibbly Wobbly. It was docked near Jane's house and was a nice bar. I figured that I had been sober for long enough and treated myself to a pint of cider. We sat and chatted like we were old friends. I wasn't sure about what Jane wanted, but I knew that I wanted more from her.

Once we finished our drinks, Jane said that the dock where I used to swim was round the corner. We set off, I was curious to see if it had changed in the last few years. It hadn't, everything looked vaguely familiar. My head was swimming with memories and I heard Jane point out the spot where we shared our first teenage kiss all those years ago. I had to really work hard to decipher that as I was caught in the memory of our kiss and for a moment wasn't sure if she'd asked me to kiss her or not!

As I was still looking about, I asked Jane what we should do now. She looked at me quizzically and said "I don't know, but it's getting late". While she was speaking, I was building up my courage. I looked at her, my heart in my mouth and blurted it out; "There is one thing I want to do," I drew a deep breath, "I want to kiss you."

There was a silence and we just looked at each other, I leant forward and gently took hold of Jane, our lips met and we kissed. She had the sweetest taste imaginable and I didn't want this kiss to end. But we had to breathe and the kiss ended. We looked at each other, then silently walked back to the car.

Jane drove me home, there was no conversation but she didn't seem upset or unhappy. I however, was ecstatic. Kissing Jane was like a dream come true for me. I think I remembered our fumbling teenage kisses too! And we drove in a comfortable silence until we reached my house. Jane looked at me and I could have spent forever lost in her gaze. She quietly said "I enjoyed it tonight", and I nearly cried with happiness before replying "It was perfect". We both leaned forward and kissed again before I got out of the car.

I stood in the driveway and watched her drive away before heading indoors.

Imagine a host of voices, all whispering that people are only feeling sorry for you, that you are a brain-damaged waste of space, that you aren't a proper person because of your injuries, that no one could love an idiot, that Jane's too good for you, all she feels is pity. That was the constant background sound inside my head. I may have decided not to kill myself, but it did not stop the depression and dark, low feelings from existing.

The next day at work I was worried that Jane would leave me, she was a beautiful young woman who any man would be proud to have at his side. Her planned holiday to Cyprus was getting closer, and I had visions of her being chatted up by all the lads there on holiday. I knew that I felt so much better when she was near, my personal demons would quiet down. I needed to know that she was with me, so in the middle of the day I telephoned her and asked her to be my girlfriend. Jane giggled and said that she would think about it and speak to me that evening. I knew that "will you be my girlfriend" sounded as if it had come from a fourteen year old boy, but it was important to me and that's where my brain was at.

The rest of the day flew by and I couldn't wait to get home and talk to Jane again. I had to stop myself from calling her up straight away as I didn't want to be over the top and pestering her!

I sat down with a mug of tea and waited for the phone to ring. It really wasn't that much later when Jane called me and said that yes, she would be my girlfriend. I was so relieved that she'd said yes; I think my grin met itself at the back of my head! After chatting with Jane some more, I decided to go and see Alan. I hadn't seen him for a while and wanted to share my good news with him. I think I talked his ears off, but he was glad to see me so happy and wanted to meet Jane too.

It was a fantastic feeling to have friends, family and a girlfriend who liked and loved me, brain injuries and all. Not everyone was as nice though.

Chapter Thirteen

It was now pretty obvious that my bike riding and racing days were over. I was sad about that, despite everything I still loved motorbikes. Motorbike racing is an expensive hobby, I still had my old MZ race bike and it was worth about six hundred pounds. I figured that as I wasn't able to ride it any more that I may as well sell it. Wanting a quick sell, I offered it at a reduced rate to the people at work. Neil, a mechanic, who'd I never really liked, said he'd buy it for three hundred pounds. He was friendly enough about it and we agreed that he could pay me in a couple of installments. I was beginning to think that I'd misjudged him and instead started wondering about what I'd spend the sale money on (it ended up going on a laser-engraved glass block Ducati ornament and taking Jane out!).

Neil however, soon made his true colours known. He was doing my old bike up, and being quite arrogant about my lack of modifications to it, saying that I should drop the price. I told him no and said that he'd have to pay the agreed price. As he walked away muttering to himself, I distinctly heard the words "brain-damaged" uttered. I should have said something, but I had always hated confrontation since the accident so silently seethed about it instead.

Later, I had to get Neil some parts for the bike he was working on. As I put them on his work bench, he said "Thanks brain damage". I walked away; angry and upset. The next day at work continued with Neil making jibes every time we were alone. I knew it would be bad when the first voice I heard was Neil's, greeting me with "Morning brain damage". I don't know why Neil thought it was ok to bully me like this, but it was bullying based on a disability, and my brain injury had affected how I dealt with stressful situations. I swallowed my anger down and asked him not to call me "brain damage". I think I may even had said please. Neil took no notice.

The rest of the staff and mechanics started arriving, the usual shop banter and jokes about traffic jams and tube delays. Neil kept quiet until our coworkers Des and Marcus had left. "Your special bus wouldn't have this problem brain damage". My anger bubbled up and I left the workshop, I felt only a blistering, white-hot rage and wanted to teach Neil a lesson. My brain may have been injured but I could still plan, and I knew that all I had to do was wait until eleven o'clock when Neil would be on his own. I wanted to see him suffer. I wanted to see him dead. I knew what I had to do.

Walking to the stock room, I got some parts that Des and Marcus needed. I also got a mini-axe that I'd kept there from before my accident. I hid the axe in a carrier bag, and walked the parts over to Marcus before heading over to my workstation and putting the bag to one side. Princess was there and he looked at me quizzically, I am sure that he could see the rage emanating from me. He asked if I wanted a cigarette and a chat. I barely had time to say no before Marcus came in asking if I was ok. He'd been concerned by my silence when dropping his parts off. I muttered that I was fine, but Princess told him to tell Neil to stop teasing me about my brain damage. I wondered if it would work.

I think Marcus had a word with Neil. Just before eleven o'clock, he wondered in to get some parts and said something. Neil was standing very close to me and whispered "Brain damage" in my ear so quietly, I could barely hear it, let alone anyone else. As I visualised the axe burying itself in Neil's head, he walked away. He was smiling.

Reaching to the carrier bag, I went to grab the mini-axe, but suddenly Princess's hand was on mine. We were struggling for the axe, I wanted blood. Neil's blood in exchange for every word, every sneer and arrogant put-down. Princess and I struggled for a few seconds more, until he disarmed me with one sentence:

"What about Jane? Who's going to look after her?"

I froze, my grip on the axe handle loosened and Princess got it away from me. It was as if reality bitch-slapped me. I had been prepared to murder another human being, just because he was a dick. I walked outside in a daze, automatically lighting a cigarette. One of the sales team, a young guy called Mark, and Kevin the shop manager had seen me and Andy struggling, and asked if I was ok. Princess told them that he'd warned them that I'd hurt Neil if he didn't stop tormenting me. He added that he was going to have a word with Des about it.

Princess now had to stop Mark from killing Neil. I don't know where he found the strength to hold Mark back, but he did. Marcus and Des had heard the commotion and worked out what had happened. The next thing we knew, Neil was pinned to the ground by Des! Kevin the manager eventually restored peace by sending Neil home for the day.

Nothing more was said to me about what had been going on, in fact it was never mentioned again as they didn't want to upset me. It was quite surreal how within the space of five minutes, Neil was the most unpopular person at Daytona. That afternoon I treated Princess to some Thai food for lunch, as not only had he stopped me committing murder and throwing my life away, he had been there for a lot of my low, dark moments. I don't know how Princess found the strength to stop me as he was lighter than me. Maybe he was just stronger on the day, maybe some very small part of me let him win, knowing murder is wrong.

I wanted to keep busy, my new relationship with Jane now accounted for a fair few evenings a week and I would still go and see Alan. One of my dad's friends had a son who had been blinded in an IRA[2] terrorist attack. He'd been in the Army Cadets when a bomb planted by the IRA exploded. The publicity surrounding his story meant that every so often, companies would send him gifts and event tickets, as it would be good for their corporate image. He had been offered four VIP tickets for the World Superbikes at Brands Hatch. His mum, knowing how much I liked bikes, asked me and Dad along too.

It was good timing for me, the Superbikes weekend coincided with Jane going to her cousin's wedding so I wouldn't have time to mope about and miss her, well not too much anyway! I wasn't sure how I felt about seeing a bike race, but after speaking to Jane, I got more excited about it. I couldn't wait to go to work and tell my mates. I'd be at the Superbikes in a VIP suite! I couldn't believe it - even Neil came to speak to me about it. He was very careful not to upset me, but as Princess said "he's shit-scared of Des"!

Soon Superbike Sunday came, me and Dad were excited about watching the race. Driving to Brands Hatch we saw thousands of motorcyclists heading to the Kent track too. We entered Brands Hatch via Scratchers Lane. One of my aunties lived nearby and I had a sudden flash of memory. I remembered riding up and down the lane on my bike.

[2] Irish Republican Army - a terrorist organisation (now disbanded) opposed to British rule in Northern Ireland.

The nostalgia had a sadness attached, but I soon managed to shake it off. We were at Brands Hatch!

The VIP route was one I wasn't used to following. There wasn't a lot of traffic, just a few big and expensive looking cars. And my dad's black cab! The signs for VIP parking lead us to Clearways, where we met with Dad's friend and her son. I remember looking at him and thinking that with his obvious visible disability, he had it easier than me. No one could see the thoughts that tortured me, the gaps in my long term memory and the jumps in my short term memory.

Watching the racing cheered me up and I was caught up in the excitement of it all. I had another flash of memory, I remembered my last race day here and the speed and joy of the ride. The realisation that I would never do that again brought me down. I needed to speak to Jane. I stepped outside the VIP suite and called her. Just hearing her voice on the end of the phone made me feel better. Jane told me about her cousin's wedding and the reception. She also said that her cousin's friends thought that how we got together was really romantic and an amazing story. I don't know, but I think this is when Jane realised how special our relationship was.

As I stepped back into the VIP suite, our call over, I realised that I was falling in love with Jane. I knew it was too soon to say anything to her, I didn't want to seem over-eager and scare her off. It didn't stop me from wanting to shout my love from the rooftops though!

Chapter Fourteen

Jane's holiday was getting closer and I was sad at the thought of her being away for a couple of weeks. Normally I would have spent the time with Alan, but he was now working in his family's building business alongside his dad and brother. This left him very little time for socialising, so I had gotten used to spending more time with Jane.

How I viewed working at Daytona had changed too. Motorbikes had been the focus of my life so so long and now, I couldn't ride them. Daytona was now just a poorly-paid job. My main perk of being able to buy cheap parts had gone. Now, my job was a just a reminder of who I used to be.

Before I knew it, Jane's holiday had arrived. We had agreed that we would telephone each other while she was away, and I made sure I knew what her return date was. I took Jane to Peckham Rye train station and stood on the platform with her. While we waited for her train, we chatted about how much we enjoyed each other's company and that we were both looking forward to seeing each other again. I tried to keep my inner demons quieted. They were trying to insist that Jane would find someone new, someone better in Cyprus.

As the train approached the station, I felt like I did when I first asked Jane to be my girlfriend. I looked at her and blurted out "I love you Jane". I was instantly worried that I'd said too much, that it was too soon, but Jane instantly replied "I love you" and got on the train. It was like something from an old black and white movie. Jane on the train, me on the platform, our hands pressed to the glass of the train door, and the pair of us crying with happiness. We loved each other!

With Jane now safely on her holiday, I decided to keep myself busy by redecorating my bedroom. The wall next to my bed was covered in photos of motorbikes and old friends. As I took the pictures down, I felt sad but thought of it as closing one chapter of my life and starting a new one. I also realised that I wasn't too fond of the yellow paint on the walls. Those pictures had covered a lot of ugly paint!

I was up early the next morning and headed to the DIY centre to get some paint. As soon as I walked in I saw someone whose face I knew and remembered, I just couldn't place him. He obviously knew me and stopped to say hello.

"I've read on Friends Reunited that you lost your memory, what can't you remember?"

"I don't know what, I can't remember or I would remember it." It was my stock reply and it usually raised a smile as I often got asked what I couldn't remember. We chatted for a few minutes more before parting ways. I never did work out who he was!

I returned home with tins of blue paint and a few other assorted bits and bobs. It was quite exciting, transforming my room. Doing away with the old Kev. I had been given a double bed by my sister, but had never got around to assembling it. So I put it together and bought a new mattress. By the end of the day, my room was blue and my single bed was replaced with a double bed. I really felt that a new chapter of my life had started.

Every night I would speak to Jane on her mobile phone. She would ring and before we knew it, hours had passed as she lay by the pool talking to me. She talked to me about chatting with her friends, the places they had been and the fun they were having. It was wonderful to hear her voice. When the phone bill came through at the end of the month, it was nearly four hundred pounds. We laughed or we would have cried! The time without Jane was ok but I felt lonely. I would see Alan but it was not the same. The bond between me and Alan had changed as I now had somebody in my life who was more important than him.

My Dad, a taxi driver by trade, acted as taxi driver for the family too. Dad's cab! He had agreed to collect Jane from the airport and drop her off at my family's house so we could see each other before she went home later. I sat in my room listening to the radio. I was trying to keep my mind busy, I half-feared that Jane would arrive and say she'd met someone else. It wasn't long before I heard the familiar noisy diesel engine of the taxi pull up out front.

I jumped up and ran downstairs to the front door and out into the front garden. Jane was getting out of Dad's taxi and we had our movie moment. We stopped and looked at each other and time seemed to slow down. In my mind, I remembered Jane as beautiful. To my eyes, in the flesh, she was stunning, her caramel skin tanned by the Mediterranean sun and her eyes glinting green in the sun. Then time started again and we ran to each other, I caught her up in my arms, holding her close and we kissed. I knew my fears were groundless. Jane wanted me.

The months passed and our relationship flowered. We were inseparable and I felt so loved and safe with Jane that I wanted to shout it from the rooftops. I did in a way that I never imagined possible.

Chapter Fifteen

Friends Reunited had a success story section on their website. It featured friends who had successfully reunited. In the November 2002, Jane emailed them with our story. I thought it was a nice thing to do and then thought nothing more of it. The story went up, but I barely noticed. A few other people did though. It wasn't long before Jane had a call from a press officer at Friends Reunited. They thought our story was amazing and had been in contact with a national breakfast television show called GMTV and they wanted to feature us!

Jane was dealing with Friends Reunited and GMTV by email, and before I knew it, a date had been arranged for us to go on GMTV and be interviewed by Lorraine Kelly. By now, my coma dream feeling was in my past, but this didn't seem real. Celebrities were on breakfast telly, not motorcycle accessories salesmen from Peckham!

The day of the interview arrived and we were up very early. It didn't take long for me to get ready, I just had to have a quick shower and get dressed whereas Jane had really long, tightly curly hair to wash, dry and style. My skinhead took a lot less maintenance! Eventually we were both ready by the time the car arrived. Yes, they sent a car for us. It was like being a celebrity.

We arrived at the television studio, it was near Waterloo Bridge. As we walked in, it suddenly started dawning on me that millions of people were about to see me. I started to feel nervous, but kept my cool. I didn't want to ruin this for Jane. As we walked through the studio complex, I was surprised at how many people were there, camera operators, sound recordists, runners and assistants. Another guest was wandering about and Jane got quite excited. I didn't have a clue who he was but Jane did; it was Ronan Keating, one of the members of the pop group Boyzone. The look Jane gave me was one that clearly said that I should know who he was!

We met with one of the production team who briefed us on what would happen during the show and what time we would be on the sofa with Lorraine. I asked the production assistant if GMTV would make a donation to the Headway charity. Headway had supported me a lot in the early days after my accident and I wanted to help them in return. GMTV didn't pay guests, but they agreed to make a donation and put a link to Headway on their website so viewers could donate too.

Before I knew it, we were both whisked away to separate areas of makeup. I didn't think I needed any, but everyone on telly has to have at least a bit of powder as it stops the skin reflecting studio lights and looking too shiny. As I was sitting there, I noticed Lorraine Kelly heading over to me. She was as friendly and as bubbly as she appears on television. She said that she thought my story was lovely and how she couldn't wait to interview us. Lorraine added that she'd been excited about our story since the production team told her about it a few days before!

At that moment Jane rushed over. I don't think she actually noticed Lorraine Kelly standing there. She was too excited and blurted out "We spoke about our story and he said it was beautiful, he was getting his make-up done beside me!" Jane had barely stopped to breath and I managed to work out that she was talking about Ronan Keating. Just then, Lorraine was called away and said to us "Enjoy it, we will have a ball!"

It was almost time for our segment of the show. On the studio screens, Lorraine's image froze as the show went to a commercial break. The set was a sudden hive of activity. A make-up artist rushed over to touch up Loraine's make-up and we were shown where to sit, which camera to look at and then the countdown to the end of the break began. I sat there gripping Jane's hand for comfort and support as GMTV's theme played. Before I knew it, Lorraine was giving several million viewers the background to our story, before turning to us and asking us questions. I took charge of the interview, with Jane adding bits in, and thought that I did very well. When I saw the footage back, I thought I should have left it to Jane. I did a horrendous amount of blinking and my responses were stilted and erratic. I was not used to being the centre of so much attention! Before we knew it, the interview was over and I thought so was our five minutes of fame.

We were getting ready to leave the studio, as we were both quite hungry and now I didn't have to worry about spilling food down my front, breakfast was an appealing idea, when Lorraine Kelly rushed over. She grabbed us in a friendly hug. As she let go of me she said "You have an amazing girlfriend, and you have such a strong spirit. I think you'll be together forever. And let me know how this love story goes, I'm sure it will be more amazing than anyone can imagine. Keep in contact!" With a final smile, she rushed back to the set. The GMTV show had to go on.

As we sat waiting for the taxi that would take us home, a runner appeared. He had two copies of the interview on video for us, a permanent reminder of our first, and as I thought at the time, only time in the spotlight.

Christmas was fast approaching, I decided to treat Jane to a romantic getaway as my present to her. She certainly deserved it! I knew that she had always wanted to visit that city of romance; Paris. I did some research on weekend breaks there but I needed to know a few things, like whether Jane's passport was valid and what its number was. I needed to tell some very convincing lies to her and hope that she forgave me when she found out.

The most plausible reason I came up with was booking a weekend train trip through England up to Scotland, but that the organisers required travellers to have a valid UK passport. Jane was perplexed, but convinced by my story. Her work colleagues questioned it when she told them, but I had the details I needed to book the Paris trip.

As soon as I could, I rushed to the travel agents and booked the weekend away. After reading some brochures, I decided on the Atlante

Garden Hotel, the description of the subterranean entry and huge chandeliers were brilliant and I imagined the look on Jane's face, how amazed she would be when she saw it. The hotel was well situated and not too expensive. This was good as I also wanted to get tickets for the show Moulin Rouge. The show is traditionally Parisian and I knew Jane would love it. So I booked advance tickets for that too.

I came so close to letting the cat out of the bag so many times. I was actually grateful for my memory problems as I had a cast iron excuse for any inconsistencies in my cover story. Jane later said she had suspicions, but that she couldn't work out what I might have planned. That is one of the few times I was grateful for the brain injury!

For Christmas, I was staying at Jane's house. It wasn't just me, Jane and her parents. Her brother was staying there too. He was yet another Andrew, but to me he was Fish. I was glad of this as I already knew at least two other Andrews! Andrew has Downs Syndrome, but that did not get in the way of him enjoying life to the full.

Christmas morning arrived and we all gathered in the living room by the tree. Jane rushed in and eagerly looked under the tree for her present. The present pile was unchanged, apart from a new card from me. It was the last thing she opened, her face changing from puzzled and curious to absolutely joyous and then she leapt up, cuddling me tight and laughingly referring to my cover story with "England to Scotland!" I just looked at her and said with a straight face, "Well, it is a train trip..."

Our trip to Paris was romantic, it was like every cliché imaginable. Admittedly our room was small and the view was of the building opposite, but we didn't care. Paris was beautiful and looked magical, covered in snow; like being in an old black and white movie. Our trip to the Moulin Rouge was amazing. Jane was transfixed by the show and the dancing. I was transfixed by the really tasty chocolate-filled crepes they served.

All too soon we were back at home and back to reality. But Jane got the drop on me with our next trip away. My birthday was approaching, and as it got closer Jane told me to make sure that I'd booked a long weekend as she'd booked us a break in Cornwall. And to avoid the six hour drive, we would be flying there and back, and hiring a car from a rental place there. She had really thought of everything!

It was a really relaxing weekend, we walked around and saw the sights and ate at several very nice little restaurants. The hotel was amazing, it had an old, underground entrance on the beach. This was so boats could drop their supplies off quickly. I wondered if smugglers had used it hundreds of years ago! We got a really nice photograph of it, I am positive that I took the photo, and Jane is positive that she took it. The gateway and the view beyond really spoke to me and seemed symbolic of my life, struggling with my brain injury and looking out to the future. That is the book cover image.

Once we were back in London, Jane wrote me a short poem to go with the photo. It read:

> *As I look through this open door*
> *Confusion lays in my heart no more.*
> *In you I see endless possibilities;*
> *A chance to create life-lasting memories.*

Chapter Sixteen

It is scary, realising how much of an impact one person can have on your heart. As time went by, I decided that I wanted to marry Jane and I really hoped that she felt the same way about me. I decided that I wanted to be very traditional about the whole thing, which meant asking Jane's father George for his permission to marry his only daughter.

It wasn't the easiest thing to get George on his own when Jane was out of the house. A couple of times, I popped round when Jane was meant to be at work only to discover her at home because she'd switched her shifts. I was able to blame turning up on having memory problems and getting my dates confused, my good old brain injury to the rescue and covering for me again.

Eventually, I managed to go round to the Peart household and find George there alone. As he opened the door, he said that Jane was at work. He looked confused when I said "Good, it's you I need to speak to George." He ushered me in and we went and sat in the living room. We made small talk for a couple of minutes, weather and football, while I gathered my courage and asked him for his permission to take his daughter's hand in marriage. George looked stunned and slightly uncomfortable. After all, this if nothing else was proof that his little girl, his only daughter was a grown woman, ready to leave and start her own family. He looked at me and in a quiet voice said "You have my permission."

I was elated. All I had to do now was actually ask Jane to marry me. And I wanted this to be the most special event of our lives so far. It had to be perfect, the most romantic gesture I could make to the woman who meant so much to me. I eventually settled on a plan that was romantic and elegant, while harking back to our early days hanging around Surrey Quays and swimming in the docks. I booked a river cruise along the River Thames. The boat had a band playing light jazz and I pre-ordered a two course dinner for us. When I told the cruise operators what I was planning they agreed that we could have a table near the front of the boat and wished me luck!

I had got the proposal venue sorted, and knew that I would propose as we passed under Tower Bridge. I now needed a ring for my fiancee-to-be. I wasn't a big jewellery buyer, so I asked Dad where the best place to go was. He suggested that I try Hatton Garden. It is a small area of London that has more jewellers than you can shake a stick at. I spent an afternoon visiting all the shops before I found The Ring. It wasn't just any ring, it was white gold with a bright diamond. There were rings with bigger diamonds in, but there was something about the way this diamond caught the light that moved me.

Jewellers assess diamonds by something they call "the four c's". They stand for carat, cut, clarity and colour.[3] The diamond on this ring outshone some bigger diamonds that were there, it was flawless. The ring was white gold, that was Jane's favourite precious metal, and mine too. I had a white gold bangle that I'd bought many years previously with the small inheritance my godfather left me. I was enchanted and luckily for me, the ring was in Jane's size.

My family and friends were as excited as I was. I think for Mum and Dad, that they saw this as the next big step in my recovery and rehabilitation. Alan was just excited for me, he thought Jane was lovely and that we worked well together. Me, I thought Jane was the best thing to ever come into my life.

The day of the proposal drew closer and I was getting more nervous. Jane knew that we were doing a dinner and jazz cruise, but had no suspicions of anything else. We arranged to meet at the pier near Embankment tube station. I left the house, I was suited and booted, I wanted to look my best for Jane and tonight wasn't the night for jeans and a teeshirt! The ring was in my pocket and as I sat on the train, I got the ring out. It was in a small velvet covered presentation box, and I just stared at it before closing the box and putting it safely back in my pocket. A little old lady was sitting opposite me, she gave me a knowing smile and rubbed her own wedding band. I smiled back, thinking about me and

en.wikipedia.org/wiki/Diamond

Jane growing old together. Mr and Mrs Whitehead. It sounded so adult, so grown-up and serious. I couldn't wait.

I got to our meeting point just outside Embankment station, but there was no sign of Jane. I felt that familiar fear and dread start to rise, but then my phone beeped. It was a text from Jane, "I am running late" she wrote. I was just typing out my reply when she came running up. She looked quite surprised at the extra-tight cuddle I gave her. I was very relieved. We decided not to go to a pub for a quick drink, but straight to the pier instead. I really didn't want to miss the cruise!

We chatted about holidays and kept mainly to chit chat and small talk while we waited for the boat to arrive. We weren't there long before it pulled up and we boarded. I gave my name to the attendant and he started to show us to our table. We were shown to our table, I had asked for a nice table. What we were given surpassed all my expectations. We walked through the dining room. We walked past all the dining tables and people were staring at us as we were ushered to a lone table at the front of the boat, a premium spot, but with privacy. It was the best table on the boat, I was really taken with how well the cruise company had set things up. Jane was wide-eyed with amazement, her look echoing mine. I glanced around and noticed the band looking over at us.

We were seated and the champagne I ordered arrived. The jazz band was a four-piece and they played softly in the background. The weather was clear and the backdrop of London was stunning. Jane just looked beautiful. Every time I looked at her, she took my breath away. I was so proud that a stunning woman like Jane had chosen to be with me.

I had been worried that the heat of the day would linger on and I would end up a sweaty mess, but thankfully the evening was mild. The lights of the buildings lining the Thames glittered and it was all I could do not to panic and blurt out my proposal. I was busy rehearsing my proposal in my head when the waiter appeared with the menus. It is a good job I was concentrating or I would have ended up proposing to him!

Jane headed off to use the ladies' rest room. I checked that the ring was still in my pocket and some fortuitous timing occurred. As Jane returned, we were approaching Tower Bridge and the boats' lights dimmed and the band started playing a romantic tune. I honestly thought that my surprise wasn't going to be a surprise and that Jane would twig what was happening. She didn't. She just walked back to the table, probably thinking about the meal or another glass of champagne. She did not expect me to stand up and then go down on one knee. I took a deep breath and just let the words flow. "You mean everything to me. I have grown with you, you have made me the happiest person alive. You are my rock and I want to spend the rest of my life with you. Will you marry me?"

The boat was turning small circles just in front of Tower Bridge, almost pirouetting. My mind was doing the same, I held my breath waiting for Jane's reply and held out the ring. Jane looked at me and held my hand. I stood up as she replied "Course, yeah!" It wasn't the most eloquent or romantic response, but it was one straight from the heart. We stood at the front of the boat and kissed. I was jubilant, the most loving, caring and beautiful woman in the world had just said yes to me!

As we stood there, hand in hand looking at London in the twilight, a few people came up to ask if they had just witnessed our engagement, and offered their congratulations. Before we knew it, our engagement was announced on the boat's public address system and we were cheered. The band continued to play and the cruise continued towards Woolwich. As we left the boat, the crew offered their congratulations. One of the crew explained that our table had been specially set up for us, and it was in fact, the band's usual spot. It explained why they'd been looking at us!

Chapter Seventeen

While my personal life was going from strength to strength, my work life was not. I was not enjoying Daytona any more, but I still had to go to work. I sat on the bus, my favourite tunes on and smiled as I went over Blackfriars Bridge. Once off the bus, my walk to work was long enough for me to enjoy a couple of cigarettes. Getting my nicotine fix to keep me going! As I walked, I would hear the roar of my workmates' motorbikes as they made their way in.

I got into work and started browsing the internet and stumbled over a job advert for bus drivers in London. This was appealing as it would get me out of Daytona. I would miss my friends, especially Princess, but I would be away from motorbikes. I telephoned the number in the advert and asked for an application form. I felt quite happy and pleased. Just asking for a form seemed like a major achievement.

I told Princess about the job, and his view was that maybe I just needed to be away from bikes coincided with mine. He didn't comment on the bus driving part though! After I sent the form off, I only told a couple of people at work. I didn't want to let too many people know in case I didn't get the job. Mum wasn't overly happy about me being a bus driver, but she didn't tell me not to apply as she didn't want to put me off the job or finding my own path. Jane was very supportive, saying "I think it's for the best if it's getting you down at Daytona".

I was happy to find out that my application and medical had been approved by Stage Coach, the bus company. All I needed was a start date. It wasn't long before I received a letter with my start date for training. I needed to have a PSV licence to legally drive a bus. I was excited for the future, but at the same time sad at leaving Daytona. They had really helped me, taking me back on after the accident, especially as I had technically quit so I could go to Spain.

My mum's face said more than she did about the bus driving. She was not happy about it, but would let me choose my own path. At Alan's house, his mum said how Alan's dad Steve and herself met on the buses. She made it sound like a lot of fun, very different from a normal office or shop job.

Alan spoke about how much time his job was taking up, but he seemed happy with his job and life. I was happy for him. He was surprised that I was leaving Daytona for the buses, but wished me luck. Like Mum, he didn't like the idea, but he kept his opinion to himself. He knew it wasn't really for me, and maybe deep down, so did I.

My leaving drinks for Daytona were duly arranged, and among the presents I got was a DVD boxset of the classic comedy series On The Buses! It made me laugh. I realised that I had been with Daytona for four years, and now I was nervous. My colleagues were like family and I was leaving them.

I had a few days before I started my PSV training, so me and Jane decided to spend the weekend at her mum's caravan. It was on a caravan park just outside of London. Jane had often talked about it and said how relaxing it was there.

It took us about an hour to drive there. The site had some arcades, a few shops and a couple of chip shops too. The caravan was quite big inside, but I felt uncomfortable, so calmed myself with a cigarette. Jane had learned to read my moods quite accurately and knew that a low moment would follow the uncomfortableness. She readied a cup of tea for me. It took me about twenty minutes to come out of the low moment, but Jane was patient with me. Once it was gone, we could really enjoy the time we had together. And we did!

I passed my two week PSV training and soon got on the road for my very short lived career as a bus driver on the 136 bus route. My short term memory was still giving me problems and I genuinely struggled to remember the different routes. I was pushing myself to learn instead of slowly taking the information in. I rushed trying to learn too much at once, and my confidence suffered. Bus driving was not for me, so three days into my bus driving career, I quit.

The day I quit, I was meant to be on an early shift, so I had the whole day in front of me. I decided to visit London's West End. I would go there as a kid to waste time, window shop and generally just hang around. Because my head injury had knocked me back a few years, I decided to visit some of my old haunts. I even treated myself to lunch in Debenham's department store. Back in 1992, I would often have lunch there while Mum had her hair cut at the in-store salon. It was nice to reminisce.

As I waited at the bus stop for the number 12 back to Peckham, I noticed that the bus approaching was an 88. I had the strongest urge to jump on it so I did. Fate was shouting at me very loudly indeed! I had been sitting on the bus for about twenty minutes when I realised that I recognised the area I was in. It was near a motorbike shop I used to go to. A place called Metropolis Motorcycles. I hadn't been there for a few years, but I knew some people who worked there. So I got off the bus to see if they still worked there.

I walked in the door, and yes, I recognised someone. Her name was Dee and I'd known her for about three years. We weren't close, but knew each other well enough to say hello to. So we said hello and she asked what I was doing nowadays. She already knew that I'd had a bad accident - the bikers' grapevine is a speedy bearer of gossip and news - and seemed genuinely concerned when I said that I had just quit my job. She then added that Metropolis was looking for someone in their clothing department, and that she would speak to the boss. Fate it seemed, had directed me back to a motorcycle and accessories showroom.

The owner was a man called Ian. He called me through to his office and we spoke for a minute or two. I could tell that he seemed impressed with me and seemed excited about having me on his staff. I agreed to start work the following Monday. He called out to one of the shop managers, another Andy, and asked him to get me some uniform ready for Monday.

I was very excited when I left, I was also reliving new memories that going into the shop had sparked. They were of me, Alan and Jamie going there on our scooters and drooling over the big bikes. A big red Ducati

916 stood out in my memory. Some not so nice memories came back too. I felt a rush of anger at the thought of an old friend who had take

advantage of me before my accident. It took a while to calm down from that.

My parents were unsure if getting back into the bike industry was such a good idea, but they agreed that it was better for me than the buses. They also said that I was lucky to have got another job so quickly! And at least it got me out of the house and earning a wage.

Jane was not totally surprised that I'd quit my job driving buses, but was happy for me getting the job at Metropolis so quickly. She did suspect that I'd known in advance about the Metropolis vacancy and that I'd wangled it, but I hadn't. It was just fate again.

I didn't always agree with the path fate chose for me. Sunday night was soon here and I started having doubts about working at Metropolis. I was even beginning to wonder if I was even employable, it had all happened so quickly that I hadn't even had time to think about it. And all too soon it was Monday morning.

As I walked to the bus stop, I was coming up with excuses about why I couldn't work there. I was scared of the bikes, I was unemployable, it was too quick. The thoughts whizzed round and I even missed my stop. But I thought of Jane, and how I wanted to be better for her, a better person and a better fiancé. So, I got my arse in gear and got off the bus. Sparking up a cigarette, the tobacco calmed me and I walked to Metropolis.

Bob, the sales manager was outside. He was joking with another salesman as they pushed the motorbikes onto the shop's frontage for display. He saw that I looked nervous and uncomfortable and cracked a few jokes to put me at my ease. It worked. I relaxed and lit another cigarette. "Don't worry," Bob smiled, "the ball and chain are removed for cigarette breaks." I quickly retorted "I have to chain smoke, it takes the smell of vodka off my breath!" I actually giggled and thought at least I'd get my nicotine fixes!

I went to the clothing department, I was the first person there and for a couple of minutes stood there looking a bit lost and lonely until Dee came in. She looked cold, but she had come in on her boyfriend's motorbike. She gave me a key to the staff room and said to make myself a drink while she went and got changed. I felt instantly comfortable, which was nice. I liked being part of a team. Andy came in, he was the manager of the clothing department and would be my boss. He quickly explained a few bits to me and I was ready to go!

Metropolis wasn't only a motorbike and accessories shop, it had a riding school attached. While they were waiting for their lesson, a group of students came in for a look around. Although I felt nervous, I was able to advise them on different types of motorbike gloves. The rest of the day passed quickly. I took the lead sales role, while Dee did the weekly stock check and Andy did some paperwork and other managerial work. By lunchtime I had already sold quite a bit, as if I'd been in sales for years. At the end of the day, Andy congratulated me on an excellent first day and said he looked forward to seeing me the next day.

My second day at Metropolis was very nearly my last. I had woken up with a start. I don't know what sparked my sudden awakening, but it didn't bode well for the day. As I walked up to Metropolis, I realised I couldn't cope with working there. I had been stupid. I had pushed myself too hard. I hadn't listened to the doctors or my parents or Jane. I had tried to do too much. Bob was outside the shop and called a greeting over to me, I didn't reply. I just carried on walking.

As I walked further away from Metropolis, it felt like the weight of responsibility was lifted from my shoulders. I knew I was letting people down. And with that realisation all the dark and dangerous thoughts flooded back to me. I was a failure as a person, and a waste of space. I should have died in the accident.

Dad was still at home when I walked into the house. "Why aren't you at work?" he asked just as I broke down, sobbing and crying that I couldn't cope with the pressure of life. Dad just held me as I cried. He tried talking to me, but nothing was getting through to me. As much as I love my dad, there are just some things that he couldn't deal with and an overly emotion son was one of them. He phoned my mum, asking her to come home from work.

Mum's work was close to the house, so she arrived within a couple of minutes. They talked briefly about how I needed to re-learn controlling my emotional responses. Dad had a hard time understanding some of it, but he couldn't stay long as he had to start work. Being a self-employed cabbie, Dad had to leave for work, whereas Mum had more flexibility and an understanding boss. Mum sat with me for about half an hour, reassuring me that what I felt and my panic was normal for someone with my injury. By the end of the day, I had decided that Metropolis was not for me. I was just sad at letting everyone, especially Jane, down. When we spoke on the phone that night, I didn't tell her what had happened as I didn't want her to worry. I just made up some stuff about my day; silly I know!

Wednesday morning arrived all too quickly. I gathered my uniform up and headed to Metropolis, eager to hand it over, quit and get back to the safety of home. Across the road from the shop was a small cafe. I decided to get a hot chocolate before going in. The man at the counter recognised me from Monday and asked if I was new at Metropolis. I just nodded before leaving with my drink. I really didn't want to get caught up in conversation with anyone.

Bob was pushing the bikes out for display on the pavement again. He waved at me and jokingly said "Are you sure it's not your day off today?" He thought that yesterday I'd accidentally came in on my day off. I just smiled at muttered something non-committal before going in and heading to Ian's office. I didn't take the route through the clothing department. I was too embarrassed.

When I got to Ian's office, he was on the phone but he indicated that I should take a seat. It felt like being back in the headmaster's office in school. He finished his call, then turned to me and and asked what had happened yesterday. His concern was evident to me.

I explained that I wasn't ready for work yet, that the pressure was too much and I was scared at the thought of eventually selling motorbikes. Ian listened as I spoke, letting my fears about work out. He didn't interrupt me, he just listened. When I had finished saying what I had to say, Ian replied, saying that he'd watched me and that I was a natural salesperson. He added that I had fitted well into the clothing department team, and that I had excellent communication skills and was able to adapt to individual customer's needs. My confidence rose slightly. I didn't think I'd done all that well or that Ian had noticed me. He continued that he thought I'd make an excellent bike salesman, but he understood if I didn't want that role.

Ian's next sentence left me gobsmacked. He said that I could stay working in the clothing department until I found a job that was better suited for me. I had not expected that at all. While I was reeling from that, Ian added that I could take any time off that I needed for training courses and job interviews as it was easier to get a new job while holding down a job already.

How could I say no to any of this? I don't think it was possible for any company to be any more accommodating of my needs. Ian said he'd give me a few minutes to consider the offer. I was glad of this as half of me was screaming at me to run away and hide at home, the other half of me knew that I couldn't hide forever and that this was an amazing opportunity. While I contemplated the offer, Ian called Andy, my manager in. Yesterday had been Andy's day off so he'd only just found out about me not showing up yesterday. To say he was surprised was an understatement.

Ian and Andy talked quietly while I contemplated my future. I heard Ian ask Andy what he thought of my prospects. Andy replied that I'd shown great potential and had suggested changes to the returns process which had already been implemented. I thought about about the offer Ian had made for me, how on earth could I turn it down?

Ian walked back over to me, "So," he said "giving you everything that you've asked for and helping you with future references, do you think you can keep earning me money?" After everything he had done to accommodate me, there was only one reply I could give. "Yes" I said. This was a big step for me, and really helped my recovery and rehabilitation.

As the next few months passed, I found work easier, enjoying my time at Metropolis. I still had the low moments, but they were manageable. I didn't even really look for other work as I was happy working in the clothing department.

Chapter Eighteen

I had always thought that the GMTV interview would be my five minutes of fame and I could go back to my normal life. No. It seemed that our story was one that people were interested. I was surprised to get a phone call from one of the national tabloids, it was the Daily Mail and they wanted to shoot some pictures of me and Jane, and run a story about us. It was also quite short notice, it was for later that day! I said I wouldn't be able to get out of work that quickly, but they must have really wanted the story as they said the photographer would come to me and they'd organise a taxi to get Jane from her work. Oh, and what was my collar size as their stylist would send a couple of shirts for me to wear. They were keen!

It wasn't long before Jane and the photographer arrived. Andy and the rest of the team were watching from the side, I guess it must have been weird for them to see this media attention on a salesman! Jane looked stunning, she'd already done her hair and make-up, and me, I hadn't even had a chance to wash and brush up yet. I grabbed a clean shirt from the photographer and ran to the employee bathroom to get ready. It was time for our first photoshoot.

The photographer asked us about our story while he was setting up the camera, and he was amazed by it. He even suggested that it would make a great book or film. I hadn't ever considered that before and I wondered which Hollywood stars would play me and Jane in the movie versions of our life!

The pictures and story appeared in the paper[4], and that really heralded the start of strong media interest in us as a couple. It was very odd for for me. I almost couldn't understand why anyone would be interested in boring ol' Kev, but then I would think about Jane and realise that yes, our love was special and now I had my opportunity to shout it from the rooftops. We did interviews and posed for pictures and enjoyed the ride while it lasted. Fame is fleeting, but our relationship was going to last.

From the moment we got engaged, Jane took over our wedding preparations with all the zeal and efficiency of a Sergeant-Major. Before the congratulations of friends and families had time to finish echoing in our ears, we'd already been to see several wedding venues and even went to a wedding fair.

I had really only thought about married life with Jane, I hadn't really thought about the wedding. After the wedding fair I realised why wedding planners stayed in business! From organising flowers, dresses, venues, transport, photographers, receptions to well, making sure everything runs smoothly on the day, they earn their money! Thankfully Jane was more than up to the task.

We eventually decided to marry at a small church in Hornchurch, with everybody staying at the Park Inn Lakeside, where we'd also host the reception. I didn't want Jane to shoulder all the burden of organising the wedding, so took to organising the transport. I wanted to support local businesses, so hired a local chauffeur who promptly disappeared with our deposit. I left countless messages on his voicemail and email before he finally got in touch to say that he'd double booked himself and that there'd be a delay in getting our deposit back. We eventually got our money back and Jane booked the cars and chauffeurs that she wanted! She also organised a bus to take all our friends and relatives from the hotel to the church and back again.

It didn't seem like much time had passed, but suddenly it was the night before the wedding and we were booked into the hotel with friends and family. I didn't have any last minute worries about marrying Jane, I knew

---

a www.dailymail.co.uk/femail/article-356483/Old-flames-reunited-website.html

it was truly the best decision of my life. It was just the end of one chapter and the start of a new one.

I was in the hotel bar with Dad, George and Alan. Alan was my best man and in charge of making sure that I got to the alter in one piece. It was also my first time drinking with George, and I didn't want to embarrass myself. Jane, her mum Angela and the bridesmaids all stayed at our house. We managed to speak briefly on the phone but she was busy organising everyone and everything! Jane had a full complement of bridesmaids with my little nieces Montana and Savannah, her best friend Sonia and her cousin Emma. My nephew Ryan was her page boy.

The thirty-first of March 2007 dawned bright and early. I had shared a room with Fish and he'd snored all night long. When he wasn't snoring, he'd ground his teeth! And boy did he grind them! It was actually worse than the snoring. He, along with Jane's other brother Matthew, and Alan's brother Steven were my ushers.

After breakfast, people started to get into their wedding finery and I had some time to kill. I had a nervous energy I wanted to work off and it wasn't long before me, Alan and the ushers were running round the grounds and generally letting off steam. We then had photos to do. I wished that I had Jane's organisational skills as I ran round chasing people up and getting them to different areas of the grounds for photographs. There were some formally posed pictures, as well as some fun ones, including one of me and some close friends and family running around a tree. I also had some great photos of me and Dad, they are pictures I'll cherish forever. Before I knew it, everyone was being herded onto the bus for the trip to the church.

As I sat on the bus, I looked out of the window wondering at the turns my life had taken. If it wasn't for that truck turning when it did, I would be in Spain, racing bikes and travelling the country. Instead, I was still in England, still suffering the effects of my brain injury and unable to race or even ride. But I had the most amazing fiancee, and more love than I had ever dared dreamed.

As we got closer to the church I had a brief spell of panic when I thought what if Jane doesn't show? She may be the best thing for me ever, but what if she could do better than me? I stopped that train of thought as deep in my heart I knew that Jane would arrive and I did not want a panic attack to mar our wedding day. And then we were there, at the church. For a split second I wondered if this was all a dream, but reality snapped back in when I heard a car horn toot, breaking the spell. As I stood in the church grounds with Alan and Dad, I saw the caravan of cars approach, Jane's Rolls Royce in the lead. I caught a glimpse of my beautiful bride and hurried inside.

I waited at the alter, Alan joking that this was my last chance to escape, and then, my bride entered the church. George held Jane's arm and as the church organ played the wedding march, I gazed dumbstruck at Jane, she was stunning. As she walked down the aisle, guests stood straight in the pews, their eyes trained on Jane. I was so excited; that moment before the ceremony began, for me, it was like waiting for the lights to change to green at a bike race. I even prayed, thanking God and my family for enabling this moment to happen.

The priest was brilliant, his service emphasised the bonds of love Jane and I shared and our love. I had been really nervous about the recitation of our vows, I really didn't want to forget what I was to say. Thankfully the priest broke the vows down into short chunks that I could recite and not muck up. I don't think I had ever felt so happy as I did, when I kissed Jane. Our first kiss as husband and wife.

The ceremony was over and as we walked together, back up the aisle, I looked at my family. Nan had the biggest smile imaginable on her face. I was so glad that she was able to see us marry, it wouldn't have been the same without her there. As we passed Auzzie, I mimed revving a motorbike, someone managed to get a picture of it.

Outside the church we posed for the professional pictures. The sky was clear, the day was beautiful and our families and close friends were there with us, laughing and smiling, and Jane and me started our life together. After the photographer had finished with us, we all made our way back to the hotel for the reception. The bus that Jane had organised soon filled up, and my wife and I sat in the back of the Rolls Royce. The seats were so deep that they almost swallowed us whole! The ride was so smooth, I felt I could get used to the luxury of a classic car and chauffeur.

Jane and I talked about how the wedding went, we both agreed that it was very odd seeing Auzzie in a suit and tie! As the Rolls travelled to the hotel, we saw people waving at us. It was nice to receive all those good wishes for our future.

The car pulled into the car park at the Park Inn Hotel, I noticed the bus had not yet arrived but Jane, ever efficient, had made sure there enough parking space left for it! We waited near the door to the wedding reception so we could greet the guests. I hadn't quite realised how big Jane's family was; even their supersize family parties hadn't quite prepared me! Our guests filed in and before long the DJ was playing the music for our first dance; Wonderful Tonight by Eric Clapton. It a distinct break from tradition, our second song was the ambient classic Destiny by Zero 7. In a further break from tradition, I sang along to Destiny. I think Jane would have been happier if I hadn't sung at all!

George, Jane's father, made a fantastic speech. His sister in America had helped him prepare it and he delivered it impeccably, it was the perfect father of the bride speech. Alan was next up with his best man's speech. I was nervous as anything about this. Alan had seen me do so many stupid things over the years, things my new wife and her family did not ever need to know. Ever. They especially did not need to know that in the Gypsy Moth pub, I had eaten a plate of someone else's leftovers because the serving staff hadn't cleared the table from the previous occupants. I sat there with my head in my hands, totally embarrassed, but that is the point of the best man's speech after all!

I had decided not to give a traditional speech, but instead to read a poem I had written for Jane.

Uncomparable love, proposal so sweet
Under Tower Bridge, got down on one knee
Moment of truth, yeah course means everything to me
Seeing the city glint in my eye
Next step forward of happy you and I
Snowballs in Paris, Ibiza sunshine
Smugglers in Cornwall, Casino red light
How amazing this day Jane, to think where we have been
My heart open for you, come on within
You bring happiness to me as you did from the start
We can go forward now,
Mr and Mrs Whitehead, this is our new start.

This did cause a few eyebrows to be raised, but the poem described our journey together and more succinctly and sweetly than any speech could ever do.

The celebrations ran on into the evening. Some work colleagues attended in the evening and it was great to share the good times with them. Nan told me how happy she was to be there and see me married. It meant a lot to me to have her approval and love. I sat back in a chair and watched my family and friends enjoy themselves, I had to laugh when I saw Dad hit the dance floor. My dad loved to dance and would often grab the nearest people to dance with. Once on a cruise, he had grabbed these two young woman for a few dances and they'd all had a great time boogieing. Mum had watched and laughed as Dad's ego was stoked by dancing with two pretty young ladies.

As the night drew to a close and our guests departed for their own homes and beds, Jane and me made our way to the honeymoon suite. Our first night together as man and wife and we were exhausted! We sat in our room and looked back at the day together, laughing over trivial little things and feeling sentimental and hopeful about our new life together. To top it all off, Angela, Jane's mum, had left us a box of Ferrero Rocher[5] chocolates. She really was spoiling us!

Chapter Nineteen

Our honeymoon had been planned well in advance - mainly by Jane, although I did help! We had a couple of days at home together before setting out to Australia for nearly a month. Jane had always wanted to visit Australia and I quite wanted to see it too - Jane had dismissed my suggestion of the Antarctic as being too cold! I agreed that we would both enjoy Australia though!

On 2nd April, Dad once more became our personal chauffeur and drove us to the airport. Mum came along too, partly for the ride and partly to see us off safely. We enjoyed a meal together in one of the airport restaurants, hugging each other goodbye before Jane and I went to the check-in and passport control desks.

Boarding the Qantas flight to Sydney, we were shown to our seats. We had got very lucky, we were in the front row of the middle aisle. This meant that we had at least four feet (1.2 meters) of legroom, it was like being in the first class area! The stewardess was really lovely and helpful, she seemed genuinely excited about this being our honeymoon and wished us well in our future.

As the flight went on, Jane fell into a light sleep. I just sat there, looking at her and marveling at how lucky I was to be married to such an amazing and beautiful woman. Until I needed the toilet. I made my way to the toilet, did what I had to and washed my hands. I didn't normally wear jewellery, especially rings as they have a habit of being caught in engine parts and either being damaged or damaging you. I was so not used to wearing a wedding ring, So much that I didn't realise that I hadn't put it back on after washing my hands. I just made my way back to my seat, covered up with a blanket and snoozed next to Jane.

e en.wikipedia.org/wiki/Ferrero_Rocher

The next thing I knew, it was two hours later and Jane was shaking me awake. She was in a bit of a panic, "Where's your ring?" she asked. I looked down at my hand, and my comprehension grew as I remembered taking it off to wash my hands. I jumped up and got briefly tangled in my blanket before throwing it aside and running to the toilet. Which was engaged. I stood outside for a few minutes until the door opened, the poor bloke inside barely had time to get out before I rushed inside.

Sitting there, on the side of the sink, was my wedding ring. I exhaled loudly in relief. I heard a snicker from outside and the man said that if I hadn't rushed in, he would have handed the ring to the stewardess. I was so relieved to have the ring back. It would not have been a good start to the honeymoon or married life if I had lost it!

Our hotel in Sydney was amazing. We had a stunning panoramic view of the famous Sydney Harbour and Opera House. It couldn't have been more perfect if it had tried. The hotel even had a roof-top swimming pool, which I was brave enough to use once or twice. I had expected Sydney to be hot and dry, it rained most of the time we were there, but the temperature was lovely, not too hot or too cold.

I wanted our honeymoon to be perfect, so before we'd left England, I went online and researched some of the top restaurants in Sydney. I found one that looked spectacular. It was at the top of a tower, like the BT Tower in London, and the restaurant revolved, giving diners an ever-changing view of the city. The online reviews were all glowing, heaping praise on the Michelin-starred chef. I booked a reservation online, explaining it was our honeymoon and the restaurant confirmed that they would give us window seats and were looking forward to seeing us. I couldn't help but think back to the cruise on the Thames where I had proposed to Jane.

We had both dressed up for the meal, Jane looked as stunning as she had on our wedding day. We did not want to look shabby when dining in such a high-class establishment. Our taxi was waiting outside and we left for the tower. Arriving there, I gave my name to the porter, he had trouble finding our name on the reservation list, but took us up in the lift to the restaurant. At the restaurant, we were greeted by a Chinese lady who said she didn't have our names on the reservation list, but that considering it was our honeymoon, we could have a window table anyway. We were surprised to see that the restaurant was not that busy, considering the hoops I'd had to jump through to get the reservation in the first place. Jane even wondered if we'd got the date wrong!

We had an amazingly average Chinese buffet, but the views made up for the food. I wondered if the restaurant was having a Chinese themed night, but I was disappointed in the Michelin-starred chef. How could all those reviews have been so wrong? It turned out, they weren't. I hadn't realised that there were two restaurants in the tower, and the one I'd booked was on the floor above the Chinese buffet! When we'd arrived, the porter must have assumed we wanted the buffet and hadn't bothered to check the other restaurant's reservation list!

Sydney isn't just restaurants and hotels though. On one of the few days when it wasn't raining, we took a trip to Bondi Beach - or as Jane called it 'Bondy Beach'! I had always wanted to try my hand at surfing and Bondi was the world's surfing capital. What better place to lose my surfing cherry!

The smell of the sea air as we arrived was invigorating, so fresh and clean compared to some of the beaches in the UK. We walked along the hot sands before finding a free space and setting up our towels and refreshments. We sat there, soaking up the sun and holding hands as we looked at all the people around us. Some people were sunbathing, others playing frisbee or catch. Many had taken to the sea for a paddle or swim, and others were surfing, seeming to fly over the waves.

It did not take long for the prospect of surfing to lure me away from Jane.

I quickly found a surfboard hire shop, and chose an eight-foot long novice board. The shop owner was explaining surfing technique and protocols to me, but I was barely listening. My mind was already out on the waves. He asked me about wetsuit hire, but I shut him down. It was a lovely, warm day, I wouldn't get cold so had no need for one. All I needed to do was follow the advice my dad had given me. "Son," he'd said, "staying on the board should be your first task at surfing." That was easier said than done!

I threw the board into the water and paddled out. I was surfing at Bondi! I was so excited and then saw my wave heading towards me. This was it. It wasn't a big wave, but it was mine and enough to get my adrenaline pumping. I turned my board and started to paddle away from the wave, letting it catch up with me. This was it. This was my moment. The wave caught me, I jumped up on the board and promptly fell off. Surfing is not as easy as it looks! I just hoped not too many people were pointing and laughing!

Still, as the saying goes, if at first you don't succeed, try again. So the next hour and a half was spent paddling around and falling off the board.

I got rather good at the falling part! Still, I could feel the rubber foot pads on the board starting to take their toll on my abdomen. I thought I might have got a bit of a graze from the friction, so decided to return to the beach and Jane.

As I walked up the beach, a few people looked at me and grinned. I guessed they must have seen my surfing attempts. Jane was where I'd left her on the beach, but she'd acquired a fruity cocktail, it looked like something Del Boy Trotter would not have been ashamed to drink! We sat and talked for a bit, but the sea called me back. I'd been watching the local surfers and picked up a few tips that should help me stay on the board. So I spent another two hours paddling and falling, but enjoying it. By now my stomach was quite sore, so I paddled back to the beach.

As I walked back up to Jane, the people who had grinned at me before now winced at the sight of me. I thought I must have a bit of a red stomach from the food pad friction on the board. Jane was sipping another Del Boy cocktail when I got back. "I lost to the sea!" I announced dramatically before sinking down next to Jane. Jane just looked at me, removing her sunglasses for a closer look. Confused, I looked down. My abdomen had been scraped red raw. There was even blood seeping through my pores.

"Why didn't you wear one of those wetsuits?" Jane asked, somewhat pointedly and very concerned.

"I didn't want to... It was a nice warm day and I told the hirer I didn't want one..." I felt quite daft when I realised that wetsuits aren't just to keep you warm, they are to stop you from ripping your stomach to shreds on the board! If I had payed attention to the hirer, my stomach would not be in this mess! We spent the next hour or so under one of those big beach umbrellas, the last thing I wanted to do was get sunburnt on my stomach. And at Bondi the sun is very strong. I'd noticed that all the australians applied a lot of sunblock and kept pretty covered up in the heat of the day. Sensible!

I took the board back to the hire shop, I had decided that a third trip out on the surf was definitely not going to happen.

"Dude! Are you ok?" The man in the hire shop sounded so stereotypical of an australian 'surfer dude' it was almost funny. He had the biggest wince on his face, like he felt my pain.

"I should have taken the wetsuit," I grinned ruefully at my own stupidity. He shook his head and laughed with me, and advised that I buy a particular body cream that would help with my dose of surfer's rash. This time I followed his advice.

The next stop on our honeymoon adventure was Hamilton Island. It was a beautiful place, highly spoken of in the guidebooks and it looked like paradise. We arrived at a tiny little airport and were met by a representative from the hotel. Our luggage was sent on ahead and we were taken by golf buggy. The representative was a young woman and she drove the buggy. She told us about the history of the island, how it was privately owned and what sort of facilities were available to us. One useful thing was that as the island, the hotel and the other facilities were owned by the same family, anything we wanted could just be charged to our room. It felt very luxurious and decadent!

The scent of the tropical flowers that grew wild on the island mixed with the sharp smell of the sea. The overall fragrance was fresh, wild and clean all at the same time. The buggy arrived at the hotel and we checked in. Once more we struck lucky with the view from our room. We overlooked both a swimming pool and the sea.

We spent a lot of our time hiking round the island, or sitting on the beach and watching the sea. We found a beautiful and deserted beach on one hike, and started talking about our future. The wide open horizons seemed to echo the limitless choices and options we would have before us.

The highlight of our stay on Hamilton Island was a trip to the Great Barrier Reef. This is an area of outstanding natural beauty and the largest coral reef on the planet. We went scuba diving there, and I should have learnt from my Bondi experience that when an expert tells you something, you listen and then do it. I was distracted by the sheer beauty of the reef and as a result, my scuba mask was all over the place. Naturally I could rely on my love, my life partner, my wife to point, laugh and take pictures of me looking like a total wally.

Diving at the reef was a mind-blowing experience. Brightly coloured tropical fish flitted and flicked around us, darting in and out of the coral reef. The corals themselves were beautiful, bright colours glinting in the filtered sunlight. I was stunned at the size of them, the calcified skeletons of their ancestors helping give the coral reef its size and grandeur. I was not surprised to find out that the reef is visible from space! From the reef, we sailed over to Whitsunday Island. It is the epitome of every image of a tropical island, from the pure white silica beaches to the lush tropical vegetation.

The next stop for us was Cairns. We hired a car and took drives around the area. The city of Cairns was originally a gold mining town, but because of its coastal position, soon became a major port. The city was lovely, but the surrounding countryside, with its mountains and forest was awe-inspiring. When Cairns was first discovered by Captain James Cook in 1770, he called it Trinity Bay. The Walubarra Yidinji aboriginals who had been there a lot longer had already called it Gimuy. Sadly, due to social and environmental pressures, the Yidinji language and many of their traditions are now almost extinct.

On one excursion to the nearby rainforest at Cape Tribulation, our guide was South African. He knew the area so well it was as if he'd been there all his life. He had a great sense of humour and had me and Jane in fits of laughter throughout the day. We followed ancient Walubarra Yidinji walkways through the rain forest. It was humbling to think that we were following in the footsteps of people who had walked those same paths thousands of years ago. Another day trip took us to an unexpected taste of Spain down under. Paronella Park was built in the late 1920s and early 1930s by a Spanish ex-patriot called Jose Paronella. He decided to build the park for his wife Margarita, as a taste of their Spanish home in Catalonia, and to open it to the public. In later years he added a small theatre, tennis courts and a tea garden. His story really spoke to me as I identified with his love for Spain and wanting to do anything to make his wife happy. As I looked at Jane, I realised that I would do anything for her too.

Unfortunately for Jose and Margarita, a series of natural disasters destroyed a lot of their work, and the park was eventually shut down in the 1970s. In the 1990s, new owners bought the park and began the painstaking process of restoring it to its former glory. In spite of everything, it is beautiful and a wonderful story that will always live with me.

All too soon it was time to leave Australia and start the journey back to England. We had a brief stopover in Singapore. And it rained. That combined with high temperatures made for a very sticky and humid stay! We had a walk around the Royal Botanical Gardens, which Jane really enjoyed, I was just glad to see her happy. Later we went to a shopping mall, I was so glad to be in an air-conditioned building after the humidity of outdoors! We walked into one store that sold traditional herbal remedies and massages. I chose a revitalising back and neck massage. I think it was Jane's way of rewarding me after dragging me round the gardens! I changed into the thin 'massage shirt' they offered me, and a very petite lady started the massage.

The first ten minutes were very relaxing and I was really starting to sink into a state of bliss. Then, the deep tissue massage began. For twenty minutes it felt like she was using her elbows to find every knot in my muscles, and then use her entire body weight to give extra strength to the massage. I honestly think she found every nerve in my back, and had the feeling my bike accident had hurt less. She was very surprised to find out that I hadn't enjoyed the massage! Never again. Ever.

The return journey to England continued; we were taken in a Mercedes E Class to the airport where we boarded our flight home. We didn't have such good seats this time, but we still had plenty of legroom and I took extra care when using the toilet and washing my hands. I did not want a repeat of losing my wedding ring again.

Finally, we arrived back at Gatwick and as we left the arrivals area we kept our eyes peeled for Dad. It is a wonderful feeling knowing that no matter what, your dad will be there to pick you up. And suddenly, there he was, with Mum. It wasn't really too difficult to spot them. They were the ones holding a big sign with "Mr & Mrs Whitehead" emblazoned across it. "That's us then", I joked to Jane. We were home.

Chapter Twenty

Becoming a married man was not the only big change happening in my life. I had decided once and for all to move away from the motorbike industry and was about to begin a training course to work with London Underground Ltd as a Customer Services Assistant. The first thing I learned was that they loved to speak in acronyms! So I was going to work for LUL as a CSA.

The training took place at a place called Ashfield House in West Kensington. I was really worried about my memory and had flashbacks to the mess I'd made as a bus driver several years earlier. I did not want to fall back into my old habit of panic attacks and paralysing fear, so used a mental image of Jane calmly telling me that "you can do it" to keep my morale and confidence up.

I surprised myself by getting on really well with both the trainers and the training. I was even more surprised to find myself considered to be one of the best trainees in the group! That was a real change from how I was on the buses. The training progressed, I learned and sailed through the mock test, even all the safety critical questions. Then came the day of the actual exam.

I knew I should be able to do this and as I sat through the exam, the answers came to me easily. And then I got to one of the safety critical questions and my mind went instantly to one of the choices. The wrong choice and I didn't realise. This was a question I had answered correctly only the day before. I had failed the exam. I might lose my new job and have to go back to Metropolis. I was scared to say the least.

The trainer, a man called Mo, was surprised at my error, but tried to reassure me, saying I could re-sit the exam a few days later. My confidence was shaken, but the trainer (and later Jane) reassured me. They had more faith in me than I did!

Soon the day of the re-sit arrived and I filed into the examination room with the other entrants. Mo briefly ran through what we were to expect and added that if anyone had a problem they couldn't understand, they should raise their hand and he would help explain the question. And then the test began. I fairly zipped through the questions at first until I came to one, I was certain that my instincts on the answer were correct, but I started to think and then over-think it. I pulled myself out of the thought spiral and decided to let my brain clear and come back to that question later. I continued with the exam and breathed a sigh of relief at the end. I went back over my answers and sat back, relaxed and confident.

Later, as I sat there waiting for my final mark, Mo came up to me and asked if I had run out of time. "No", I replied, puzzled, "I had plenty of time and checked back over it. Why?".

"You left a question unanswered, that's an automatic fail." Mo looked disappointed. He hadn't thought any of us would fail. That I would fail. I saw my hopes and dreams for a new career and future slide away. I saw the disappointment in Jane's eyes. I started to feel sick. "Why didn't you answer it?" he continued. I was so far sunk into my misery I didn't hear him and Mo had to repeat himself.

"I must have turned two pages at once when I was reviewing the paper," I shook my head, feeling wretched at the termination of my contract and dreams with LUL. My memory had failed me again, how could I have forgotten that I wanted to go back to the question? Then Mo gave me an unexpected second chance. He handed me the paper and told me to answer the question there and then. I looked at it and the answer sprung instantly to mind. I marked it on the sheet and then handed it to Mo.

"Congratulations Kevin, welcome to London Underground. You passed the exam!"

I was not just happy, I was jubilant!

Leaving Ashfield House, I checked my phone. I had four or five missed calls from Jane. She was eager to find out if I'd passed and knew what time the exam was due to end. The delay in me calling her must have had her on tenterhooks! I quickly called her to say that I had passed and was now officially an employee of London Underground. I cheekily added that there was a bit of a story attached to it all and would tell her when she got home from work. I knew this would get her curiosity going!

"Tell me now!" demanded Jane.

"At home," I firmly replied, although I was chuckling to myself. When Jane came in that evening, I told her and she laughed and celebrated with me. I was finally in a career away from motorcycles and it was a career I could progress in. It felt like I was a proper "family man" and I had Jane to thank for it all.

I didn't really want to work at my local tube station. Dagenham Heathway was nice enough, but I wanted to be busy and at the centre of things. I was really pleased to be assigned to the Charing Cross group of stations, in the heart of London. It was a small but busy group of stations that included Charing Cross, Lambeth North and Elephant & Castle stations. Officially I was a Charing Cross reserve, this meant that my time was split between all the stations - although most frequently I was at either Charing Cross or Elephant & Castle. My first week on the job was spent at Elephant, and the staff were very nice and welcoming to a newbie like me.

In one of those weird coincidences, I found out that Nan had worked on the tube at Elephant & Castle back during World War II. One evening, over a plate of pie and mash, she told me about her time there, polishing all the ticket office counters and keeping the ticket hall spotless. Air raids and the threat of invasion were no excuse for a messy ticket hall!

The shift work was something that I had to get used to. Dead early shifts began at five in the morning! That meant I had to get up at about half past three in the morning. Previously, the only time I had seen half past three in the morning was at the end of a really good night out! The other shifts varied throughout the roster, the latest shift beginning at five in the afternoon. I really had to plan my family and social life well in advance!

The tube is a quasi-official slang term for the London Underground system.

The other LUL staff came from all walks of life, and many were people that I would never have met in my old career with motorbikes. There were staff from all over the world, heavy metal fans and calypso lovers, well, just about the widest range of people working in one place that I had ever seen. But everyone was really nice and friendly, and that was the most important thing. I became really good friends with a few of the staff, especially a woman called Violet. I valued her opinion on a lot of things; she took me under her wing and really looked after me in those early days. I ended up calling her 'Mummy Violet' because of her mothering nature.

I had only told a few people about my accident and the media interest. I didn't want to be seen as bragging about it - although most of my stories did end "thankfully I could blame it on memory loss"! One or two people that I told even suggested that my story could be a movie and asked who would play me!

A year passed by very quickly. My life was still going well. I was with a fantastic woman who I loved, I had a good job and I was coping well with things. My depression would never completely vanish, but it was held at bay and I had several coping mechanisms in case it did try to rear its ugly head again. A lot of my memory was still patchy, but I was more concerned with the present than the past. Jane and I had decided to extend our little family and have children.

One day at work, I got a message to call Jane urgently. She had good news that couldn't wait. I wondered if she was pregnant and raced upstairs so that I could get a mobile phone signal and call her back. I stood in Trafalgar Square, my heart pounding. Surely only pregnancy was the only reason for a message like that. No. It was only another publication interested in our story! Oh well. We had already been mentioned in The Sun and The Metro[7].

The magazine in question was Woman, it had been around for decades and was one of the UK's biggest selling magazines aimed at women. I spoke to the journalist who had contacted Jane, and she was very excited, promising a double page spread, my approval before publication and of course payment. The last part was the most interesting part for me; the hallway needed redecorating and supplies don't come cheap!

Less than one minutes later, my mobile phone rang again. This time it was a press agency. I don't know why, but when one magazine or paper

~ www.thesun.co.uk/sol/homepage/news/1771943/Memory-loss-Kevin-Whitehead-finds-wife-10yrs-on.html www.metro.co.uk/news/339349-memory-loss-biker-stumbles-across-wife-on-friends-reunited

takes an interest in you, they all do! This agency said that they had a client who were a "glamorous, stylish magazine" (which will remain nameless for now) and were interested in featuring us, even though they weren't a chat magazine. This magazine usually featured high fashion and international celebrities! That didn't impress me, but the idea of a bidding war (and my hallway) did. I told them that my story was currently under offer with Woman and how much for. The agency named a price. I said I'd be back in touch.

Jane and I were both highly excited, this could be brilliant but we had to decide not only on the money, but who would do a better story. In the end, Woman offered us double the agency's offer and the agency's client took back their offer of featuring us, as they didn't normally do human interest stories. So we went with Woman.

Woman sent a journalist, photographer and stylist to the house. It was great to see Jane being pampered and dressed up to the nines! The magazine took the story more from Jane's point of view and it was nice to see her in the spotlight as without her, well, I don't know where I'd have been. As promised, we had approval on the article and it was amazing. It was a double page spread, with photos of us as a couple and in our younger days too. Our fee came in and the hallway was redecorated. We even had enough left over for a few meals out!

Publishing the article reignited the media interest in us and I spent a fair bit of time turning down offers from agencies, magazines and even the local paper! The money from our story would have been nice, but we had other things on our mind. Jane was pregnant and we needed a bigger house.

Chapter Twenty-One

Sonia had been one of Jane's bridesmaids and had recently moved to a place called Leigh-on-Sea, near Southend-on-Sea in Essex. I didn't know the area at all, but Dad had spent time there as a young boy, going to the cockle sheds with his aunts. He had loved it and his enthusiasm rubbed off on me. I decided to seriously consider Leigh-on-Sea as a future home.

There were a few things to consider, like the commute and local schools. The schools in the area all had a good reputation. I wanted my children to have the best education and start in life possible, and not to miss out on their education like I had by bunking off and getting stoned. The commute to Charing Cross was lengthy, and would involve trains, taxis and my car on early shifts, but it was manageable.

One Sunday, we drove to Leigh-on-Sea for a look around the area, and to get an idea of what type of properties were available. It was lovely, having almost a village feel to it and right on the seafront. It couldn't have been more picturesque if it had tried!

On the way back home, we drove through a place called Chalkwell, and I noticed a Chinese restaurant. Suddenly my mind dredged up a memory. I was sitting in that restaurant with Alan, we were laughing and joking and there was a third person with us. I just couldn't see their face or remember their name. I knew that would bug me! And it did. I really wanted to remember on my own, to exercise my mind, but after five or six days I just gave up and phoned Alan. "It was Tim," explained Alan patiently, "he lived there and we went out for a meal together." As Alan said that my memory kicked in and I remembered Tim!

We chatted a bit longer about Leigh-on-Sea and before I could stop myself, I commented on how "it would be a great place to bring up children". Me and Jane hadn't announced the pregnancy at that point. We wanted to have the first scan done before saying anything. Alan knew we were trying for a baby though, and just assumed I was talking about the future!?

The following weekend, me and Jane returned to Leigh-on-Sea for more house-hunting. Jane was still in love with the area, but I was concerned about the lack of car parking. Some houses did have drives and garages, but they did cost that bit more. While Jane was engrossed in estate agents' windows, I had another flashback. It was 1999 and I was in

Tenerife with Alan, we met a group of lads from Southend. It was a good memory but I had to drag myself away from it to look at potential new homes. I looked at the range of photographs in one estate agent's window and one leapt out at me. "That's nice" I breathed, and dragged Jane inside to ask the estate agent about it.

The house had virtually everything we wanted, off-street parking, good sized rooms and a garden. It was about half a mile away from where we ideally wanted to be, but it was only half a mile! That's nothing in the grand scheme of things. It was just out of our budget though, but I wondered if the seller would agree to lower the price. "Well," said the estate agent, "it had been sold but the buyer changed his mind at the last minute. The owner is willing to drop the price for a quick sale though."

Quickly conferring, Jane agreed with me that we should go and view the property. The agent phoned the owner and we set off to see the house. It was nicer than the previous properties we had seen, and even the door number was perfect for Jane - it was the same as her late grandmother's door number. Fate was working with us again.

The owner was a man called Nick. He seemed really nice, and was very easy to get on with. He showed us around and the house was exactly what we'd been hoping for. To us, it looked like it was in perfect condition and I had a good feeling about it, as did Jane but we would wait for the surveyor's report. Nick was very easy to talk to, and we all talked about the house before wandering off-topic and chatting about anything and everything.

As we left, I said that we would be in touch with the estate agent about a second viewing. Nick smiled and handed me a card with his phone number on, saying that we should just call him directly to arrange the next viewing.

On the drive back, Jane was flowing with design ideas for the house. Imagining something like that, all those colours and patterns, was something that I couldn't really do any more, not since the accident. Jane was certainly the boss in matters of decor and decoration. I just did what she told me!

Once we got home, I called Alan. I wanted his professional advice on the house and asked if he'd come with us for the second viewing. He agreed straight away, curious to see the house that I was already in love with. I then called Nick up, asking if it was ok to bring a builder with me for the second viewing, and he agreed. We set a date and time for the following weekend and it was sorted!

In the meantime, there was something even more important happening. Jane's first scan. We still had not told friends or family about the pregnancy. We sat in the hospital waiting room, our hearts racing with excitement at the thought of seeing our baby on the ultrasound monitor. And then after what seemed a lifetime of waiting, our names were called. The examination room was crammed with hi-tech equipment, and as Jane lay on the bed, her belly still relatively flat, the ultrasound technician observing the monitor screen started smiling broadly, "It looks like twins are the order of the day."

I looked at Jane in shock. She had the same look on her face. We got the technician to repeat herself. We were having twins! We looked at the monitor and there they were. Two funny little bean-shaped blobs, our babies. It was still too early to tell the gender of each child, but I did have a hankering for a boy and a girl. One of each. And to my eyes, Jane lying there, her belly covered in gel and our babies in her, she was never more beautiful.

The journey home was quite strange, I thought that I would be jumping for joy, but we were rather subdued. Twins, it would be hard work, and I would need to get the house sorted sooner rather than later. I was going to be a father and I had to be able to provide for my family.

Both sets of parents were elated, their excitement bubbling up. Jane's mum said we would definitely need a bigger house. We agreed! Mum had an inkling about our news, she had had this conversation with my sister more than once and recognised the look in my eyes. Our friends were over the moon too, especially Alan. Auzzie was typically reticent, muttering something along the lines of "it's about time".

I had heard that singing and talking to the babies while they were still in the womb would help them get used to voices other than their mum's. So every evening, I would snuggle up with Jane, and sing and talk to her belly. The song I most often sang was one my nan had sung to me when I was little. I think Jane must have got tired of me singing 'You Are My Sunshine', but I sang it to our babies regardless.

I took Alan to view the house. He loved it too, mentioning that there was no way we'd have been able to afford such a nice period house in London, especially a detached property. Nick let us in and gave us free range to look around, saying he'd be pottering in the garden if we needed him. Being London lads, we were shocked by this level of trust. We'd never let someone just look around our homes like that!

Alan liked the house, he noticed a few small problems, but said it would have been odd if a house of that age didn't have a few issues. I arranged for a surveyor to visit the property and waited for the report. It took a few weeks but eventually arrived. The report said there was a bit of damp, so I got a specialist to have a look. He said it wasn't a major problem but it would cost about two to three thousands pounds to fix.

So time passed. Buying a house is not a quick process, and it was taking its time. Meanwhile, Jane's belly was expanding and our babies were growing rapidly. On the nights when I had to work late, Jane's brother Fish would sing to her belly for me. He even learnt all the words to 'You Are My Sunshine', which was brilliant considering his Downs Syndrome.

Because Jane was carrying twins, she had to have more scans than in a normal pregnancy. Twins and other multiple births have a higher risk of disability, so we had to seriously discuss what to do if a serious disability was found. The first disability checked for was Downs Syndrome. Jane's brother had it, and we both agreed that we would not terminate any of our babies over that.

At a later scan, the gender of one of the babies was obvious. He was definitely a boy! The technician asked if we wanted to know the gender of the twins, so we said yes. She scanned Jane and said "Two boys." I was shocked as deep down I had wanted one of each, and had thought that is what Jane was carrying. Then the technician said "Oooops... I scanned the same baby twice. You have a son and a daughter. And they both look perfectly normal and healthy."

Jane was ecstatic, I was ecstatic, our smiles could not have got any bigger. I even started singing 'You Are My Sunshine' to Jane's belly. I am sure the technician thought I was mad! I don't know what the babies thought.

Chapter Twenty-Two

I didn't realise how long it takes to buy a house. It seemed like forever, waiting on surveyors' reports, solicitors and banks to write letters. And the babies' due date was getting closer and Jane was getting larger still. Jane was still holding down a full time job, as well as planning and organising the move. All that and every night, her womb was home to the most rocking disco in town. The babies would go wild when I sang to them. Some friends said it was because they were trying to escape from my singing. Honestly, I couldn't blame them if they were, but I wanted to be sure my little ones knew their daddy's voice.

Then it happened. We had the completion date for the move. It was in the same week that Jane was due to give birth! Not the best timing, but at least we had a date. On one of my days off I went to Leigh-on-Sea to pick up the keys for the new house. I was surprised that Jane came with me as she was due to drop at any moment. But she would have hated missing out on anything and there was no way I could have handled all her questions about it if she hadn't come along.

On our way home, we stopped off for a bite to eat. The babies were taking a lot of Jane's resources, so she was always hungry. As we sat there digesting our meal, Jane mentioned that she felt a little bit tight across her belly. We put it down to too much chicken. I dropped Jane at home and then went to work the late shift at Charing Cross.

Jane had been booked to have a planned caesarian section. The way the babies were lying would cause a lot of problems if they were left to have a natural birth. We did not want to risk that. I called Jane during my lunch break (which on a late shift is at about half past nine in the evening) and all was fine.

Just as I had given the last tube train of the night the green signal to go, my radio crackled into life. It was my supervisor Joe Thompson, a well-known wind-up merchant. He said I had to ring Jane's mum as it was urgent. "Oh yes", I laughed to myself, "You don't know I spoke to Jane four hours ago. She's fine." I sauntered back to the operations room to hand in my radio for the night, I was spinning the radio in my hand as I walked in the door.

" Call Jane's mum " Joe looked anxious and my heart leapt into my mouth. He hadn't been pranking me. I hoped to God that I hadn't missed the birth. I called Angela. "Jane's being taken to St. Thomas's hospital," she explained, before adding that my dad was on his way round to take her to the hospital. Even before I had finished the call with Angela, I was working out how long it would take me to run to St. Thomas's.

As I started to gather my things together, Joe said "I'll drive you there". I headed for the exit with Joe following closely behind me, he hastily grabbed car keys jangling loudly. By car, it is a very short journey to the hospital, barely three minutes. I was about to become a father, I was excited and scared all at the same time, I felt sick with nerves and anxiety.

Because Charing Cross is so close to St. Thomas's, I was the first of our family there. I stood near the ambulance entrance into the hospital, looking at each new arrival, hoping to see Jane. I was worried in case I was at the wrong hospital or if Jane was delivering en route. Eventually I saw Dad's taxi pull into the hospital grounds and it was closely followed by the ambulance Jane was in.

I rushed to her side as we were admitted to the emergency unit. She was lying in bed, looking perfectly calm and relaxed. I was a panicky mess! Then came the word, the delivery suite was ready for us. It was full of people, I could not believe how many staff were needed for what was meant to be a routine procedure. I must have looked worried as Jane had to reassure me, "There are two babies, so they need two teams.

One for each baby." Thankfully, my concerns were brought to an abrupt halt by the arrival of the surgical assistant. It was not her calm presence or professionalism that stopped me and Jane in our tracks. It was that she was the spitting image of a lady from work! From her bleached blonde hair and red lipstick, to her strong south London accent, she could have been Madeline's twin. If she had one!

Jane was given an epidural. It took a few attempts to get her in the right position for the injection, but she eventually had the pain relief. The surgical team raised a short curtain across Jane's midriff so that she wouldn't see the incision being made. I was glad that I was holding Jane's hand and didn't see the incision either as I am very squeamish and did not want to faint in there. The medical team were busy enough as it was!

I must have gone pale anyway as the anesthetist asked if I was ok, before inviting me to his side of the curtain. I saw my little girl enter the world, feet first. "She's out" I told Jane, as the first team rushed my baby girl to the side and started cleaning her up. And then we heard it, her first cry. She definitely had a healthy set of lungs on her! Now all we had to do was wait for her brother. He was coming out head first, covered in mucus and already crying and screaming. The woman who looked like Madeline remarked "You won't get a quiet moment with him." She was right!

Olivia Lillian Whitehead and Louie Oliver Whitehead entered the world, kicking and screaming on the ninth of March 2010.

Chapter Twenty-Three

The next six or seven months were hectic. With two babies to look after, sleep was something we both missed! We had finally moved into the house, so Jane and me were both busy decorating and really making it ours. All of that and work too. It was very tiring, and I didn't think that I could cope with anything else happening.

I was at work when a message came through for me to phone Jane. I ran up to Trafalgar Square, where I could get a mobile phone signal. Working underground does tend to mean that friends and family can't contact me, so they have to telephone the station and leave a message for me. My mind was racing and I was panicking. Were the babies ok? Was Jane ok? Was she pregnant again? My hands were shaking as I hit speed dial and called Jane.

"I'm nominated for Woman of the Year! I'm in the finals!" Jane's voice was not just excited, I swear she could have shattered glass!

"Errrr, Woman magazine haven't contacted us again have they?" I asked, puzzled.

"Kevin…" Jane was using her patient voice, the one that translates anything as "Shut up and listen to what I am telling you". She continued "It is Cosmopolitans magazine. They have an annual Woman of the Year awards ceremony and our story in nominated in the best love story category."

I was not as excited as Jane. I didn't get so excited about the media any more, but this was not about me. This was about Jane, being recognised for everything she had done to help rebuild my broken mind, giving me my life back in a way I could never have dreamed of. I did wonder how Cosmopolitan had found out about our story. I figured that the press agency I had spoken to just before the Woman article was published might have talked about us to other high profile magazines.

Feeling relieved that everything was alright, I went back to work. I had left my colleague Gary looking quite nervous and worried, so he was relieved that everything was alright as well. The only other person at work I told was my supervisor Greg. Greg knew all my background story and often commented that I should write a book or have a film made about me! He really did seem like my PR guru or manager.

Jane had passed my shift details to Cosmopolitan, as we were both needed for a photoshoot over in West London, near Parsons Green. "District line" I instantly commented. Once you start working on for LUL, the tube map is imprinted in your brain!

The day of the photoshoot arrived. Jane was really excited, and I was quite excited too. We loaded up the car, got the twins settled in their carseats, programmed the SatNav and headed for the photographic studio.

"You have arrived at your destination," the SatNav announced authoritatively. We parked up and got the twins into their push-chair and headed to the entrance. My attention was immediately grabbed by a Mercedes Executive car sitting outside the studio. It's windows were blacked out and it looked as if it was owned by a celebrity. Jane

ww.cosmopolitan.co.uk

wondered who it might belong to, I thought that it might belong to a famous finalist. I just couldn't work out who!

We gave our names to the receptionist, who telephoned through to the representative from Cosmopolitan. She arrived in reception just a minute or so later and instantly started cooing and fussing over Olivia and Louie, she thought they were adorable. She took us through to a hospitality area and offered us something to eat and drink. It didn't take long before I had a cup of tea in my hand!

There was certainly a lot going on. There were rails and rails of clothing, hair and makeup stylists rushing around, people carrying photographic equipment and lights everywhere. The twins were engrossed by it all! Nobody was too busy though to not come over and fuss the babies! Jane pointed out that someone else was having their picture taken. It was Katie Piper, she was a former model who had been raped and severely disfigured with acid. She had just launched a charity that helped and supported people with burns and scars[9]. As Jane mentioned her name, I remembered the case from a couple of years earlier. It had been horrific and I had felt really sorry for her. It was great to see her doing so well and helping other people too.

It was not long before the stylist came for us, and started getting us ready for the photoshoot. I was put into a quite tight, fitted shirt. It took me back to getting ready to go clubbing with Alan and the lads! While we were getting changed one of the Cosmopolitan staff sat with us and the babies. That way the twins got used to a strange face before being left alone with her. Louie, in particular got upset when meeting new people. Jane and me went to get photographed and we were trying not to laugh too much as we heard this stylish, high-fashion magazine staff member talk nonsense to Olivia and Louie!

I could not wait to get out of the shirt. It was ridiculously tight and I felt quite breathless from holding my stomach in so much! While I got back into my much more comfortable teeshirt, I noticed Jane chatting with Katie Piper. I sauntered over just as Katie was cooing over the twins, she had got a little too far inside Louie's personal space and he started to cry. "Oh don't worry about it," I said cheerfully, "Louie's not good around strange faces..." As I said those words I realised just how bad they could have sounded and I started to go red and just wished the floor would swallow me up! I really hoped that Katie knew that I just meant "strange faces" were just people who were strangers to him. Just as I was trying

---

9 www.katiepiperfoundation.org.uk

to work out the best way to get my foot out of my mouth, Katie was called away to do more photos.

A few moments later, one of the journalists came over. She had to write a short summary of the story and wanted to get the all the facts correct. As we chatted, I asked who would be judging the competition, thinking maybe readers or the editor. "Oh," she replied, "we have a celebrity panel lined up." I was surprised to hear that, but hopeful that the celebrities would see the amazing love and life Jane had given me. I wanted her to win, because I wanted the world to see what she had done for me.

As we were leaving the studio, we were given the date and time for the awards ceremony. I was working. Typical. Cosmopolitan magazine asked us not to mention the photoshoot and award. Jane looked at me and I looked at her. I mean, we had only told family, close friends and one or two people at work... The only person we wished we could have told was Nan. She had passed away a few months after the twins were born and was greatly missed by everyone. I was happy that she had the chance to cuddle her great-grandchildren.

It was a few weeks and I was back at work when I got a message to phone Jane. Once again I popped above ground to Trafalgar Square. I was working with Gary again, our
shifts coincided a lot! I phoned home and Jane answered straight away. I barely had time to say hello before Jane blurted out "KEVINGUESSWHATWEHAVEWONTHEAWARD!" She was as excited as a small child with a huge bag of sweets. And a puppy.

Jane explained that Cosmopolitan had called to say that we had won the best love story award. They were telling us in advance because they needed to make sure that we were both there on the night but mainly we were available on the next day too. I thought this was probably to make sure we were available for interviews and publicity shots. I had to start swapping shifts and getting time off work booked. This is difficult in many jobs, but it is even more difficult at the London Underground because staffing levels are not just a suggestion or best practice. They are a legal requirement because we are safety critical, that means we are trained in safe and effective station evacuation procedures and dealing with emergency incidents.

As the day went on, I watched the women who walked through the station carrying magazines like Cosmopolitan. I wondered what they would say when they saw my grinning mug in it, next to my stunningly beautiful wife. Would they be shocked or happy? Would they think I just looked like the bloke in the magazine?

As the awards got closer, Jane started panicking about what to wear and how she looked. To my eyes she was as beautiful as ever, but Jane was worried that she wouldn't look as glamorous as all the celebrities and models because she still carried a little bit of baby-weight from her pregnancy.

A few days before the awards, Jane was called again by the Cosmopolitan awards organiser. She wanted to make sure we were both still available the morning after the awards as we were invited for morning tea with Samantha Cameron, wife of the British Prime Minister David Cameron. Tea at Number Ten! Jane phoned me at work and once again I raced upstairs to Trafalgar Square to call her back.

"The morning after the awards we've been invited to morning tea at Number Ten Downing Street!" Jane giggled excitedly.

"Meeting John Major! Wow!"

"Kevin," sighed Jane, "It's tea with Samantha Cameron, the Prime Minister's wife. John Major hasn't been Prime Minister since the 1990s..."

There were still times when my brain injury showed through, and my brain still occasionally flipped back to 1996. But that didn't detract from how happy and excited I was. I thought about how proud Nan would be of us. I went back downstairs, I was working with 'Mummy' Violet and she was the first person I could tell about this. Even though I wasn't meant to! I couldn't wait to get home and phone Mum to tell her too. I didn't want to call her from my mobile in case anyone overheard me, and we were under strict instructions from Cosmopolitan not to tell anyone. And I still needed to get that day off work!

When I got home, I sat down with a mug of tea and phoned Mum, "Guess who won the Woman of the Year best love story?" I asked mischievously.

"Not you... Oh my you have, haven't you!" Mum barely paused for breath before adding "What do you win? Where do you have to go? This is wonderful news!"

So I started to explain about the awards ceremony, the celebrity after-party and being put up in the Thistle Hotel at Marble Arch. I then mentioned I needed the next day off work because we were going for morning tea.

"Who with?" asked Mum, "Not the Queen?"

I stayed silent for maybe a bit longer than was necessary. Mum started to say something but I cut her off laughing, "No Mum, not the Queen. But we are going with all the other award winners to meet Samantha Cameron at Number Ten Downing Street for morning tea!"

Mum paused for a moment before uttering a very unusual for her "Wow!", then saying quite gently "Your nan would be very proud of both of you." We sat there, in our respective homes, thinking about the strong and loving woman who had headed our family for years. Even after her death, she was never far from our thoughts.

Chapter Twenty-Four

Although I was known for leaving things to the last minute, I had put in a request for annual leave as soon as Jane had told me about the morning tea invitation. But the awards were only a couple of days away and I had not heard back from local management with a reply. I was concerned and Jane was panicking! I did not want to ruin her big day, and me not being there would be a definite blow.

I still needed to get the second of November off work and the official route was not looking good. Then, the union saved my life! Or at least morning tea. The RMT[10] announced that they were holding an official strike over job cuts that would impact on public safety. It was for the second of November. I have never been so pleased to be a union member! When I read the email the RMT had sent through, I nearly cried with happiness. I also nearly wore my RMT pin-badge to Number Ten, but changed my mind at the last minute. I did not want to turn Jane's day into a political statement.

A day or so later, I was working with my supervisor he came up with a great idea. He suggested that I get business cards made up, as they'd be handy at events where I would be mingling with journalists. It was a very sensible idea as Jane was already fielding lots of calls from press agencies and magazines eager for our story. I think they had sensed Cosmopolitan's interest in us.

Rail, Maritime and Transport Workers' Union

Being at work and not telling everyone was very difficult. When I was writing on the information whiteboards, I was tempted to scrawl "tea at Number Ten" across them. However, there were two people I could tell, and they were my babies. I still sang 'You Are My Sunshine' to them every day, and explained how "Mummy and Daddy are going for tea at Downing Street". They didn't understand a word I was saying, but they laughed and gurgled at me. They could certainly understand moods, feelings and love.

With the awards only a few days away, Jane began worrying. She had just realised that she would have to give a speech and the thought terrified her. Organising large scale events, such as weddings or moving house, was not a problem. Telling people what they had to do and when, was not a problem. Speaking in front of a hundred or so people was a problem.

"Kev," Jane asked, "could you do my speech?" It was unusual for Jane to ask me to do something instead of her, so I knew it was a big deal for her.

"Of course," I replied. I could do public speaking, no problem. I had MC'd to jungle music in my teens. This wouldn't be too different. I already had ideas swirling around my brain about what I could say. After a few minutes Jane asked what I had come up with. I just grinned and refused to say anything. If what I was planning worked, this would be a speech to remember and I didn't want to spoil the surprise for Jane.

The awards arrived quicker than I could believe. It really seemed like time had flown by. I'd arranged to meet Jane at Marble Arch tube station, so made my way there from work. I'd had to dash from Charing Cross to Aldwych to pick up my suit from the cleaners before going onto Marble Arch. I had a fresh shirt for both the awards and morning tea, but needed a tie still. Thank goodness every large train station has either a Tie Rack or Tie Shop in it. I think it must be the law!

It was as I was running round London, dragging my wheeled case behind me, that I realised I was one of the 'trolley brigade'. I had always been a bit dismissive of them, as often they didn't seem to care where their cases were or who they tripped up. But today, with my trolley and my suit in its protective cover over my arm, I looked like a fully fledged member of the brigade!

I made it to Marble Arch without losing the case, the suit or myself. My biggest fear had been leaving something on the tube and really upsetting

Jane. As I got to the street level, my phone chirruped at me. It was a text from Jane, she was already at the hotel and wondering where I was. I walked quickly to the hotel and flashed the doorman a quick smile, before scouring the lobby looking for Jane. Then I heard Cosmopolitan's representative's voice in my ear.

"Hello Kevin." I jumped at the suddenness of her appearance, before settling down and exchanging polite small talk. She continued "So are you ready for tonight?" I nearly answered "No" as a joke but I saw Jane lurking in the background and I thought better of spoiling her award, so said I was looking forward to it. Jane came over and joined us, listening intently as we were given the itinerary for that night and the next day. There was not a lot of time to spare so we had to be on the ball.

We got up to our room and started unpacking. The room was nice and clean, but wasn't anything exceptional. Jane looked at the clothes I pulled from my case. "Kevin..." she said, awfully calmly, "where are your trousers for tomorrow?" Jane fully expected me to say that I'd forgotten them.

"I can wear my suit trousers again," I explained, "It's only an awards ceremony tonight, not a big party."

Jane didn't say anything, she just sighed and lowered her head, concentrating on her own unpacking. I didn't understand why she was so upset, I had saved on lugging extra clothes around town. Besides, I had a clean shirt for the morning. It just needed ironing as it had got creased in the case, but I could do that in the morning. There was no need to rush! I quickly got ready and sat back to relax with a cola while Jane got ready. She always took longer than me, but she had more to do with her hair.

We were about to leave, when Jane quickly popped back into the bathroom to do a final check on her appearance. I was still drinking from my can of cola and made the decision to pop back to the mini-bar and pour some vodka in it. I reasoned that it would steady any nerves I had, not thinking about the other, memorable occasions where vodka had played a strong part. I downed my drink, Jane was ready and we went to meet our car.

It was an experience, we had been allocated a chauffeur-driven BMW Series 7, and we were sharing it with Katie Piper from the photoshoot day. She seemed to have forgiven me for my unintentional faux-pas at our first meeting. She had a friend with her too. I didn't think about the celebrity aspect of things at all, and offered the front seat to the ladies.

Celebrities travel in the back of the car, it's the red-carpet way. Jane accepted the offer though, wanting room to stretch her legs out. So I ended up in the back with the two other ladies. I was not displeased!

In the back of the car, Katie and her friend talked about their clothes, the celebrities they expected to see and other girlie things. I wasn't really involved in the conversation.

I did keep a check on what I said as I did not want to risk upsetting Jane by blurting out something weird or stupid. My sense of humour only really worked if you knew me well. As we got closer to the awards venue I got more excited. At one point we were stopped at traffic lights and passers by recognised Katie from the television show she had done the year before. It really brought it home that I was sitting with a celebrity!

And before I knew it, we were at the awards[11]. I jumped out of the car and instantly went to the front passenger door to escort Jane out. I felt like a body guard or close protection officer! The cameras flashed their lights at Jane, before being distracted by Katie and her friend getting out of the car. I took that moment to whisper quietly to Jane that she was my "Woman of the Year".

Katie waited for Jane, and they walked up the red carpet together, the paparazzi getting as many shots of them as possible. After posing for more pictures, this time for the national press, we were directed to a small bar area with some of the other winners and their partners. We didn't talk too much at all, we were just overwhelmed by it all!

We started chatting to a lady called Meghan Fleet. She was there with her boyfriend Ed, having won the award for Ultimate Friend. When her best friend had been diagnosed with cancer and was undergoing chemotherapy, Meghan had shaved her head in support of her friend, so that she didn't suffer baldness on her own. I hit it off with Ed straight away, he looked a bit like a former West Ham player - I just couldn't remember which one!

---

www.cosmopolitan.co.uk/lifestyle/ultimate-women-of-the-year-awards-winners-
9074

Jane and Meghan were soon deep in conversation, so I hit the bar with Ed. I was pleasantly surprised to see that they were serving cider so we got a pint each, stood there and people-watched. We hadn't been there long, before an announcement was made, the dining suite was ready for us. I took Jane's hand and we made our way up the grand staircase to the dining suite. There were so many tables, I felt lost for a moment, but Jane spotted the seating plan so at least we knew where we were sitting. All we had to do was find it!

Jane and I were walking round the tables, peering at the numbers on them when a small Australian man asked if we needed any help. I assumed he was a waiter, and he helped us find the table. "Here you are!" He sounded so happy to have helped us. I said something about good waiting staff, he smiled and bounced off saying "Have a great night."

I turned to Jane to say how nice I thought he was when she just looked me dead in the eye and said "That was Adam Garcia from Strictly Come Dancing, he's a celebrity judge!" Jane giggled even as she was saying how embarrassing I could be! Trust me to be so daft!

We sat at our table, and were soon joined by Meghan and Ed. We sat there people watching. I spotted Angela Griffin, I'd had a bit of a crush on her when she'd been on Coronation Street, a popular soap opera. We also saw Fearne Cotton, Donna Air and Konnie Huq. Everywhere we looked, there was another face from the telly! Joining us at the table was Leyla Hussein. She had won Campaigner of the Year for her work on highlighting the horrors of female genital mutilation - also known as female circumcision[12]. It was something I had never heard of before, and as she explained it to me, I felt so glad that my little girl Olivia was safe from this barbaric torture. Leyla was a truly inspirational woman working hard to protect so many others.

While we were waiting for the menus to come round, I had drunk a few more drinks. This was not a good idea and Jane hissed at me to slow down on the drinking as I still had a speech to give. A speech I had spent ages writing. A speech that was sitting safely in the hotel room. I patted all my pockets to make sure, hoping it would magically appear, but no. It stayed in the hotel room near the mini-bar. I forced a smile on my face, and didn't say anything to Jane. I did not want to worry her even more. While we sat there, Jane pointed out who all the celebrities were. There were pop singers, television presenters and actors there. Some were there to present awards, others to receive them.

---

[12] www.dofeve.org/index.html

As the awards were read out I was astonished at some of the acts of bravery, courage and inspiration I heard. They really made my struggle seem quite minor in comparison and I felt like I didn't belong there. But for a love story, there was nothing that could beat our love story.

Jane was talking to a man sitting beside her at the table. He was a soldier who had received numerous injuries while protecting medics on the battlefield. I overheard him speaking and recognised similarities with my own injuries. He had suffered brain damage. It made his personality rather forceful and made people feel uncomfortable. They weren't being mean or nasty, it was just discomfort. It made me feel very lucky to be as 'normal' as I was, despite the occasional memory lapse. He didn't stay sitting with us too long, as he was circulating the room, wanting to talk to as many people as possible.

The alcohol had definitely affected me, I started getting a bit weepy as I thought about how lucky I was and how much I loved Jane and our babies. Jane, however, handled my tears like she always did. She had seen me get weepy before big events before and knew that I just had to get my emotions down to a manageable level, there was still the speech I had to say! I held Jane's hand under the table for comfort and security.

Then it was here. The final award of the night. The award for the Best Love Story 2010. Two men from the telly were taking turns in building up our introduction.

"When people fancy a change, they change clothes," said the first presenter, It was the waiter!

"Not countries!" joked the second man. They finished the build-up saying "A first love came back into Kevin's life through the accident to recreate Kevin as a person, our winners for the Best Love Story are Jane and Kevin Whitehead!"

I was out of my seat like a Jack-in-a-box, and heading to the stage. Jane was a tad more stylish and dignified, her long black dress enhancing her beauty. She took her time getting to the stage, the crowd was clapping and cheering for us. It was an amazing feeling, almost overwhelming. When Jane got to the stage, she got a kiss on the cheek from both men. In true Kevin-style I asked where my kiss was. Jane was mortified and the presenters looked a bit embarrassed too. Maybe the vodka hadn't been my best idea!

I was handed the microphone. I took a deep breath, reminded myself not to gabble and began my speech;

> "Thank you Cosmopolitan for this opportunity to share our amazing story and this chance to meet such heroic people and some celebrities..."

Then my mind went blank. My prepared speech that I had worked so hard on vanished from my mind. I didn't freeze or get stage-fright. I just opened my mouth and let the words flow out.

> "I have heard such amazing stories of people who have saved thousands of lives. Well, Jane hasn't saved thousands of lives... She saved one life. Mine. And that's why I love her."

I grabbed Jane by the waist, pulled her close and kissed her passionately. All I heard was a loud "aahhhh" from the audience before Jane pulled back from me. And as I looked into Jane's eyes, I heard the audience begin to clap, slowly at first as if they were just coming out of a trance and then thunderously. The applause did not stop until we were seated back at our table. A fitting and uplifting note for the awards ceremony to finish on.

We all moved backstage, the room was being cleared for the after-party, and we were needed for more pictures. There was even a passport-style photo booth. We didn't need asking twice, we were in there, Jane looking glamorous and sexy, me pulling faces and sticking my tongue out. As we stood there, people came up to congratulate us on the award. It was weird being the centre of so much attention.

We noticed one man standing nearby. There was a horde of girls surrounding him, wanting their photo taken with him. It was Olly Murs. He was a finalist on the television talent show X-Factor. He spotted us and headed over to say hello. He nodded hello to me and started talking to Jane. Jane did not object to this at all! I was already chatting to a woman called Fiona who worked at Cosmopolitan. I had been telling her that I had started writing my story and she was giving me professional hints and tips.

Jane only ended up spending a couple of minutes with Olly before his fans besieged him again. As he left, he reached past the girls, held Jane's shoulder and said "Goodbye, it was lovely talking to you." I could see the sincerity in his eyes. He really did mean it. While Jane was star-spotting, I had found the bar. And they were serving peach schnapps. I get very silly on peach schnapps, but the vodka and cider floating round my system told me that peach schnapps was a great idea!

At that moment, the word came that the gift suite was open. Big companies donate gifts to events like these so that the attending celebrities can be seen with their products. Jane and Meghan decided to blag there way in, asking me and Ed to join them. We declined, feeling it would be rude to leave the fully stocked bar. There was still more peach schnapps to be drunk!

The room had thinned out a lot as a lot of people had gone to the gift suite, but a few people came up to say hello and congratulate me on the award. I saw Cher Lloyd, also from the X-Factor, Jane's brother Fish was a fan of hers, I managed to get a few words with her and she seemed like a lovely girl. I recognised one of the other people as an actress from a popular telly show. She explained, quite drunkenly, how lovely my story was and how lucky I was to have found a love like that, before giving me a huge kiss on the lips! I was very glad Jane wasn't there as I said goodbye to the actress. She would have been rather upset!

After a few more drinks, I found a sofa and sat there people watching and then dozing drunkenly, while waiting for Jane to get back. I remember thinking to myself that I wished there was a dance floor there, not realising I was sitting about three or four meters away from the dance floor.

The next thing I knew was Jane shaking my shoulder and asking if I was alright. I muttered something about being bored while waiting for her, but she knew me better than that, she knew I was wasted! We decided that it was time to head back to the hotel, so a taxi took us back to the hotel. It took nearly twenty minutes to make it to the door with all the people we passed offering congratulations or asking if I was alright. I suppose I looked quite tipsy...

Jane had been busy in the gift suite. It took three trips to get all her boxes and bags into the taxi. "You've git a lot of bags remarked the driver."

"She would have taken the chandeliers if they were any lower," I laughingly replied. This got us all laughing and we made our way back to the hotel, all the bags and boxes making our room look like Santa's grotto. My final thought as I collapsed face-down and fully dressed on the bed was "what a lovely night".

Chapter Twenty-Five

"WAKE UP!!" I jolted awake, still fully dressed from the night before. I looked at Jane, bleary-eyed and hungover.

"Breakfast?" I muttered.

"There's no time for breakfast!" Jane was rushing around the room, "We've overslept and have to leave in ten minutes. The only reason I'm awake is Mum phoned!"

This was not good. My suit trousers were rumpled and stained from the after-party!, my clean shirt was still creased and I had the beginnings of the worst hangover in the world. And to make it all worse, there was no time for even a quick mug of tea. While Jane was getting her things ready - and doing a better job than me, I realised all I had to wear were my blue jeans and the creased shirt. I had the world's quickest face wash and pulled my clothes on, hoping my jacket would cover the worst of the creases.

I was barely decent before the telephone rang. It was the front reception to say that our car was there and waiting for us. As we ran to the lift, we saw some of the other award winners too. At least we weren't the only ones running late.

The lady from Cosmopolitan greeted us in reception, saying she'd heard that my speech stole the show. She then looked at me, taking in my pale face and rumpled clothing. "I don't need to ask if you enjoyed yourself," she smiled. Jane just stood there, she was not impressed with me! Jane looked very presentable and smart. I don't know how she managed it, but she looked great!

We all piled into the car for the journey to Downing Street. A few people said they noticed that I got drunk rather quickly. Leyla said she'd spoken to me towards the end of the night and although I was slurring my words, I was still pleasant company. In my defence, I had been up since half past three in the morning for work before going to the awards. The conversation soon moved onto how much Jane had got from the gift suite. She laughed and said that one of the celebrity guests had been so impressed by our story that she'd blagged her in as well. I asked who, and it turned out to be none other than my old crush Angela Griffin!

Jane proceeded to tell everyone about my crush on Angela, and added that they had planned to sneak up on me and Angela was going to pinch my bum. I looked at Jane in surprise and cursed my drinking. I could have had my bum pinched by Angela Griffin, but I was asleep on a sofa instead.

As we got closer to Downing Street, the woman from Cosmopolitan briefed us on the security measures and protocol we would need to follow. I had visions of picture of me throwing up outside Number Ten splashed across the newspapers. I could imagine the sort of dressing down Nan would have given me!

The taxi dropped us about fifty meters from Downing Street. Since the 1980s, cabs haven't been allowed to get close to the entrance of Number Ten for security reasons. It was the height of the IRA bombing campaign on the mainland, and they favoured car-bombs as they weapon of choice. We walked up to Number Ten and entered through the famous black door. It was bigger than I thought it would be.

Because of the high security levels, we all had to bring our passports for identification. I laughed to myself thinking it would be funny if I still had the same 'curtains' hairstyle as I sported in my passport photograph. I remembered going to America on holiday with my parents when I was in my teens and remarking that you could just walk through their checkpoints. At which point customs were on us like, well, anything! They went through our luggage with a fine-tooth comb. I did not want to upset Jane, so I kept my mouth firmly shut.

Once we were past security, our jackets were taken and hung away. My creased shirt was now firmly on display as we were shown to a sitting room. I saw Radio 1 disc jockey Reggie Yates, he had been on the judging panel for the awards. We chatted briefly about the awards, he said he'd looked for me at the party, but when he found me, I was asleep on the sofa. I looked sheepish and laughed.

It was then I spotted my salvation. I was hungover and hadn't eaten since the day before. It was a plate of chocolate bourbons next to a large pot of tea. I was already on my second cup of tea, before most people were halfway through their first cup and going through the biscuits like they were going out of fashion. The biscuits were good, but the tea was not so good. I prefer a stronger brew, but it was better than nothing.

I was on my third cup when Jane nudged me. The official who had escorted us into the room was back. He stood by the door and said "May I introduce Mrs Cameron." Everyone stood as she entered the room, you could hear people's posture improving instantly. Everyone stood but me. I was not trying to be rude or make a point, I was just busy trying not to throw up. But as Samantha Cameron sat down, so did everyone else and I didn't look too out of place.

We all sat together and each of the winners told their story. Samantha Cameron knew how to put people at their ease and the conversation flew rapidly by. It got quite emotional, no matter how many times you hear certain stories, it still brings a tear to your eye. By the time the conversation turned to Jane and me, I was on my fifth or sixth cup of tea and well into double figures on the biscuits. They were very nice biscuits.

Jane and I told our story, and I added that in the grand scheme of things it didn't have the impact of the work of the other ladies. I was thinking especially of Leyla's work, but Samantha interrupted me saying she thought our story was very moving, and very touching. I was so shocked at her personal interest in us that I just blurted out "Honestly, I didn't think I would last this long after my accident, but thanks to my family, including Jane, I am here now."

There was a moment of silence while everyone digested what I had admitted. I munched another biscuit. Then Samantha broke the silence saying that our story would make a good film. "Yes," I agreed with her, " I am writing a book, I am so lucky to be alive and have Jane in my life".

Samantha suggested that we all have a quick break before the group photographs were taken. Meghan and Ed came over to chat with me. Meghan asked if I had planned my speech last night, but I said no, it was just spontaneous. I kept a careful eye on the waiters, they were restocking the bourbon biscuit plates. I don't think they'd ever seen a guest demolish so many biscuits! Before I knew it, it was time for the group photographs. As the winners lined up with the Prime Minister's wife, I stood back and watched. Jane was really the award winner, not me, but I got called over to join the line-up. I looked a bit out of place, the only man among so many women! Then some of the judges, including Reggie Yates, joined in the line-up so I wasn't so out of place any more.

As we left, Samantha said goodbye to everyone individually and thanked us for coming to tea with her. She and Jane spoke about motherhood for a few moments, and she encouraged me to keep writing. We stopped on the steps for official photographs, and I saw the paparazzi at the main gates trying for a good shot of us all. While some of the other winners were having their pictures taken, I approached Reggie and asked if he'd mind getting a few pictures with Jane. He readily agreed and happily posed with her. After a couple of shots he put his arm round her, "Easy mate, she's married" I joked. His response was to pull her in even tighter for the next picture - he certainly had a good sense of humour and was a really approachable bloke!

As we left Downing Street, I remember thinking to myself about how proud Nan would have been. I wondered how my life would have turned out if I hadn't been in the accident and had reached Barcelona. Jane had definitely made my life a happy accident.

Dad once again had agreed to be our driver and arranged to pick us up from the hotel that afternoon. We had been dropped back there and quickly run to the nearest fast food restaurant! I got the largest box of chicken nuggets they sold, plus fries, milkshake and an ice-cream. I was ravenous! Jane ate nearly as much as me, as although she wasn't hungover, she had missed breakfast too!

It was good to see Dad when he arrived at the hotel, even though we had only been away for one night, it had felt like we were on a different planet. He couldn't believe all the bags and boxes of freebies that Jane had got at the event. Even the hotel porters thought we had gone mad doing our Christmas shopping!

Our first stop was with Jane's mum Angela. She had been babysitting for us and we both missed them. I hadn't realised just how much I would miss not singing with them. 'You Are My Sunshine' had become a ritual bonding moment for me with the twins, and was something I looked forward to every day.

Fish was home when we got to Angela's. We sat down for a quick cup of tea and recounted our adventures - for Fish the most important part was meeting Cher Lloyd and telling her what a big fan he was! I even reenacted my speech including the kiss! But most importantly, we were back with Olivia and Louie. They had been asleep when we arrived, but awoke at the end of my speech. It reminded me that you can have all the awards in the world, nothing is more important than being a good father.

I walked to the cab with Dad, to unload it of all of Jane's goodies, when he turned to me and started explaining how it still surprised him that I was still here, how he was still able to talk to me because on the day of my accident, he thought he'd lost me forever. My dad was a joker, not a man to talk about his feelings so this really floored me. I gave him a quick hug, and as he got into his cab, he looked back at me and chuckled "Happy accident".

I ran into the house, "It's going to be called Happy Accident!" Angela look confused, as did Fish.

"He's talking about his book!" Jane called out, busy with the twins.

"Oh," said Angela, "It sounds like a film."

"Don't get him started..." sighed Jane.

Chapter Twenty-Six

It was bliss waking up in bed with no hangover. Jane was already up and listening to a voicemail message on her mobile phone.

"Hello, this is Radio Essex. We have been in contact with Cosmopolitan magazine about the award you won, and we would love to feature you this morning, talking through the award night. If Kevin is available, it would be good to speak to him, but not essential."

"Charming," I commented. Laughing, I added "Now you have the award I don't count." Jane knew I was only joking and laughed too. She called the station back and agreed to go on air with them. Radio Essex said they would call us back, so we sat and waited for the phone to ring. The phone rang and Jane answered. We had it on loudspeaker so I could hear it too. Jane was waiting for her cue as the DJ told the listeners about our story before introducing Jane. Jane paused, just for a split second and then told things from her perspective. The DJ was very interested in the awards ceremony and the celebrities and Jane chatted about them, my ears pricked up when she mentioned Angela Griffin!

The DJ then asked to speak to me. Jane passed the phone over to me, her expression clearly saying "Do NOT do anything embarrassing!" After getting so drunk at the awards, I was determined to be on my best behaviour. Thankfully the first question the DJ put to me was a familiar one; "So Kevin, what did you forget when you woke up after the crash?"

"If I could remember that, I would not have lost my memory." My stock reply fell easily from my lips. I recounted the fun I had had at the party and mentioned some of the celebrities I had met, and then talked about tea at Number Ten. "Mrs Cameron was lovely and put us all at ease, but the tea wasn't that good..." The DJ laughed and we continued chatting for a few minutes, before it was time to say goodbye.

The call ended and I could sense Jane staring at me. "The tea wasn't nice, what are you like Kevin?"

"That's just silly old me," I grinned back at her.

Life continued for us. We still got occasional media interest and I spent my spare time writing. It was difficult going over some of the more difficult areas of my life, but writing it was really cathartic and helped me sort my own mind out.

I was still working at Charing Cross tube station. It was a Saturday morning and I popped above ground to get breakfast in McDonald's. It was still really early, but the place was busy with revellers from nearby nightclubs getting a much-needed snack. As I queued for my breakfast I heard someone shout "It's Olly Murs!" And it was. He was at the counter ordering a muffin, and already people were waiting to grab pictures and autographs.

As he left, I got my order and walked after him. "Olly," I called out, he stopped and turned round, thinking I was another fan. "I don't know if you remember me..." I began but he stopped me.

"Of course I do! Cosmo best love story! It's a great story, how is Jane?" I was really touched that he remembered us, especially as all I wanted to do was to say thank you to him for the time he spent with her.

"She always mentions it when she talks about the awards night, it's her Olly moment." I added.

"Don't be silly," Olly grinned, "I enjoyed meeting you, your story really touched me." We chatted a bit more and I mentioned my plans for a book and he laughed, "You should turn it into a movie."

"Mrs Cameron said the same thing," Olly just smiled an 'I told you so' smile, before we shook hands and left to meet his fans. Clutching my muffin, I went back downstairs to the London Underground.

Chapter 27

At the end of November 2011, Jane and me were invited out to a Chinese restaurant for dinner. We were celebrating Auzzie's brother Tony's birthday, but eventually the conversation turned to us. I explained that I was writing the book and all the encouragement I had received from people. But it was nice to be out with friends, gathered round a table and just being ourselves. Eventually the waiters came with the bill for us, and the obligatory fortune cookies. I opened mine and the little motto spoke directly to me

"Some things are more beautiful than words can tell"

The End

Acknowledgements

I cannot possibly mention all the people who by rights should be included in this book. Even if your name is not mentioned, it is not because I am not thinking of you. Every person I have met has impacted me in some way and helped me become the man I am today. So thank you, each and every one of you.

Jane, you are my rock, my world and my destiny - which I know sounds a bit cheesy, but what else could I use to describe someone who was there to support me, who gave me a reason to recover and who has always been there for me. You have become my everything, the one who my world revolves around, you have my best interests at heart. You are the girl who was always in the back of my mind, who was behind most of my choices and who I always wanted back in my life. Your also now mother to our children. And fate happened. I love you Jane.

My parents, you have been amazing all my life. I am what I am because of you, I hope I make you proud as you really were my full time carers. I hope you realise that you both did a good job raising me. Since my accident, you have been so much stronger than me, giving me the support I need. I really owe everything to you, and I hope this book makes you happy, knowing that because of you, I lived, met a wonderful woman and together we gave you two beautiful grandchildren.

Nanny Lil, A friend of a previous generation, We didn't agree on everything but I really lost a good friend. On that day I watched you leave my life happy at what jane and me had created and joined Grand dad Arthur. Final part of the family tree completed. I love you xx

Alan, you are my best mate, I sometimes wonder what would have happened if we hadn't met all those years ago, crashing your mini-motorbike into my bicycle! You have always been there, even when I neglected you during my bad-boy phase, you helped change me into a better person. We no longer speak, but your always in our mind's and I miss you.

Princess at Daytona, thank you for stopping me making one of the biggest mistakes of my life. Without you, I would not be here at all, so one of the biggest 'thank yous' goes to you dude.

I started writing a journal that became this book in the little caravan that Angela and George keep at Leysdown. I really need to get back there as it is somewhere I love being - thank you for opening it up to me. For understanding over all the years of all my difficulties, for all your support, help and patience. For everything since I got involved with your family.

And finally, this is from Jane and me to our babies;

Our Olivia and Louie, you are an amazing prize for such determination to recover by your parents. We wanted something as beautiful as you, and now realise how beautiful you are.

We hope that one day you read this story. Be it good or bad, this is our story - and your story too.

Love Mummy &

Daddy

November 2011 xx

© 2012 Kevin Robert

Whitehead

I hope you enjoyed sharing our Amazing experience with us, the book was very enjoyable to write and gave me prompts opening lots of old memory's up.

Picures are available to view at my webpage www.happyaccident-fatenotfatal.com of people from the book.

Thank you to the final person involved this, without the editorial skills of Caz Mummin the book would be "painful" to read with my basic grammar.

Printed in Poland
by Amazon Fulfillment
Poland Sp. z o.o., Wrocław